ADULT READING IMPROVEMENT SERIES

READING POWER
BOOK 3

Revised Edition

ANGELICA W. CASS

AN ARCO BOOK
Published by Prentice Hall Press
New York, NY 10023

First Edition, Third Printing, 1986

An Arco Book
Published by Prentice Hall Press
A Division of Simon & Schuster, Inc.
Gulf + Western Building
One Gulf + Western Plaza
New York, NY 10023

Published by arrangement with Monarch Press
A Simon & Schuster Division of Gulf & Western Corporation

ISBN 0-668-05970-2

Printed in the United States of America

TABLE OF CONTENTS

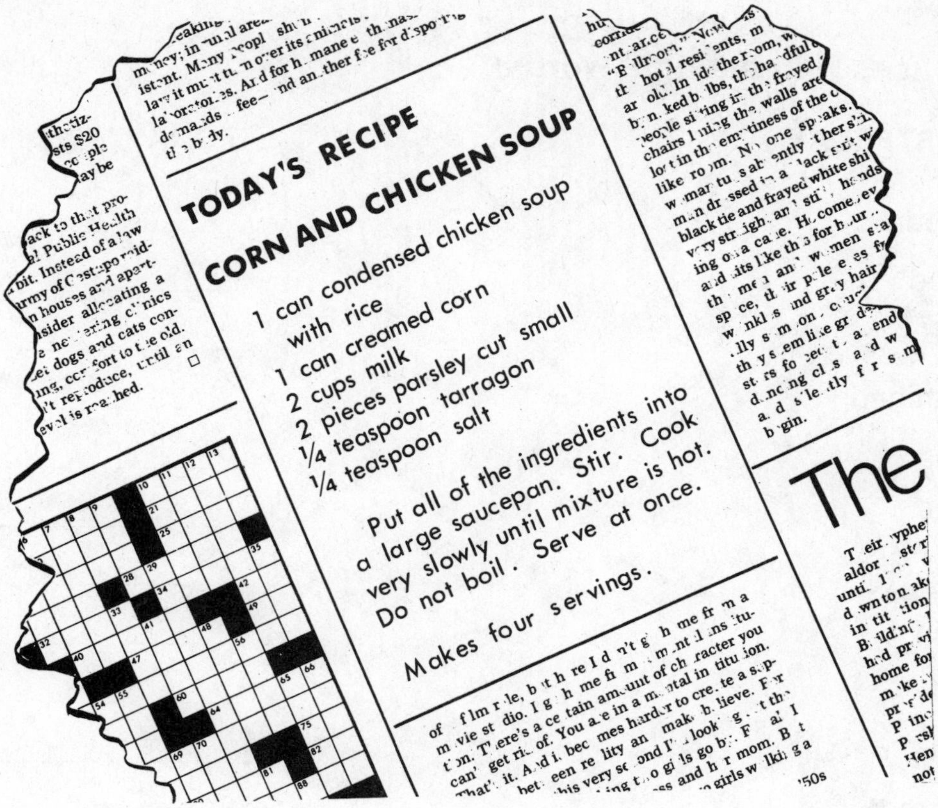
TODAY'S RECIPE
CORN AND CHICKEN SOUP
1 can condensed chicken soup with rice
1 can creamed corn
2 cups milk
2 pieces parsley cut small
1/4 teaspoon tarragon
1/4 teaspoon salt
Put all of the ingredients into a large saucepan. Stir. Cook very slowly until mixture is hot. Do not boil. Serve at once.
Makes four servings.
The

My Family Likes Soup

My family likes soup. I try to make a different kind of soup each week. Every Thursday our newspaper has a page of recipes. I watch for new soup recipes.

Here is a recipe I saw last week in the newspaper. I tried it last Friday and my family ate every drop and said it was very good:

CORN AND CHICKEN SOUP

1 can condensed chicken soup with rice
1 can creamed corn
2 cups milk
2 pieces parsley cut small
¼ teaspoon dry tarragon
¼ teaspoon salt

Put all of the ingredients into a large saucepan. Stir to mix. Cook over low heat until the mixture is hot. Do not let it boil. Serve at once. Makes four servings.

Fill in the spaces with the right words:

YESTERDAY	TODAY
liked	______________
tried	______________
had	______________
watched	______________
was	______________
saw	______________
ate	______________
said	______________
cut	______________
put	______________
stirred	______________
cooked	______________
let	______________
boiled	______________
served	______________

Arrange the letters to make words:

p s o u ______________

e c r i ______________

k l i m ______________

m y f l i a ______________

s e t a o p n o ______________

u p s c ______________

k e n i c h c ______________

p c r e i e ______________

p o r d ______________

s v e r e ______________

Write the correct words in the spaces:

ONE	MORE THAN ONE
soup	______________
family	______________
kind	______________
week	______________
Thursday	______________
newspaper	______________
page	______________
recipe	______________
Friday	______________
drop	______________
can	______________
chicken	______________
cup	______________
piece	______________
teaspoon	______________
ingredient	______________
saucepan	______________
mixture	______________
serving	______________

Put a circle around a smaller word in each of these words. Follow example:

different

for

and

can

creamed

cups

small

teaspoon

saucepan

newspaper

mixture

not

boil

once

four

rice

Check the words that are in the story "My Family Likes Soup":

___soup

___lake

___list

___drip

___rice

___cut

___smell

___pat

___hat

___lot

___boil

___at

___savings

___soap

___like

___last

___drop

___race

___cat

___small

___put

___hot

___let

___bail

___it

___servings

Write these words in the spaces:

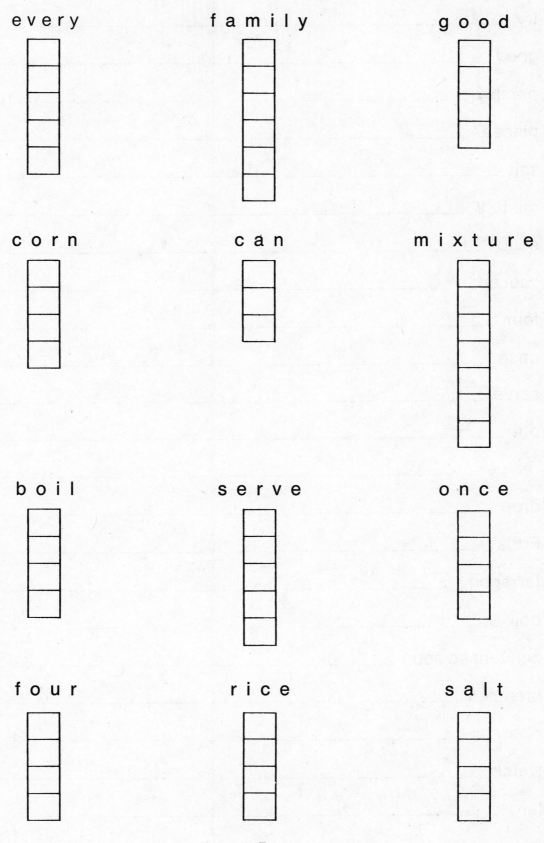

every

family

good

corn

can

mixture

boil

serve

once

four

rice

salt

Use each of these words in a sentence:

1. try ______________________________.
2. good ______________________________.
3. parsley ______________________________.
4. pieces ______________________________.
5. salt ______________________________.
6. mixture ______________________________.
7. soup ______________________________.
8. saucepan ______________________________.
9. four ______________________________.
10. once ______________________________.
11. serve ______________________________.
12. put ______________________________.
13. recipe ______________________________.
14. drop ______________________________.
15. Friday ______________________________.
16. tarragon ______________________________.
17. boil ______________________________.
18. condensed soup ______________________________.
19. creamed ______________________________.
20. rice ______________________________.
21. watch ______________________________.
22. large ______________________________.

Fill in the missing words:

My family likes ______________. I try to make a different ______________ of soup each week. Every ______________ our newspaper has a page of ______________. I watch for __________ soup ______________.

Here is a ______________ I saw last week in the ______________. I tried it last ______________ and my ______________ ate every__________ and said it was very good.

Corn and Chicken Soup

1 can ______________ chicken soup with __________

1 ________ creamed ______________

2 cups ______________

2 pieces __________ cut small

¼ ______________ dry tarragon

¼ ______________ salt

Put all of the ______________ into a large ______________.Stir to mix. Cook over ____________heat until the mixture is hot. Do not let it ______________.

Serve at ______________. Makes four ______________.

Enjoy doing this crossword puzzle:

DOWN

1. A__________tells how to make soup.
3. Adds flavor to soup.
4. Adds flavor to soup.
5. One time only.

ACROSS

2. Food to eat with a spoon.
4. Give it a go.
6. The things that make up the soup.
7. Keep an eye on.
8. Do not let the soup__________.

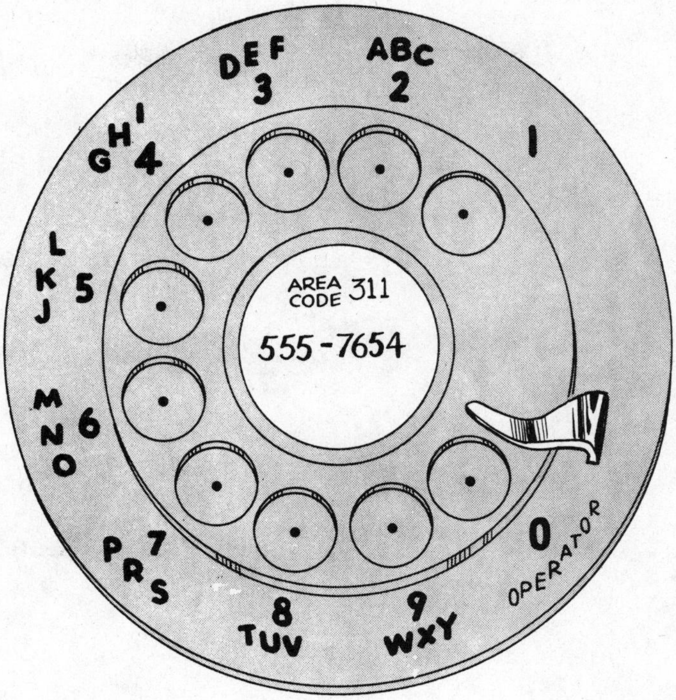
ABC
2
DEF
3
GHI
4
JKL
5
MNO
6
PRS
7
8
TUV
9
WXY
1
0
OPERATOR
AREA CODE 311
555-7654

The Telephone

Mr. Martine has a telephone in his home. He needs it for his work. His wife uses it to talk to her friends.

Telephone calls to people in the neighborhood are local calls. Local calls are easy to dial and do not cost very much.

Sometimes Mr. Martine telephones his relatives who live in another city. This is a long distance telephone call. He needs to know the area code of the city he is calling as well as the telephone number of his relatives. Mr. Martine dials the area code first — 503 — and then he dials the telephone number — 124-5687.

Long distance calls are more expensive than local telephone calls. If Mr. Martine needs help in using his telephone he dials the operator and asks for assistance.

Mr. and Mrs. Martine enjoy their telephone. They know how to make local and long distance telephone calls without asking the operator for assistance.

Check the words that are in the story "The Telephone":

___his	___has
___it	___at
___for	___far
___cells	___calls
___end	___and
___net	___not
___has	___his
___love	___live
___is	___as
___long	___song
___knew	___know
___if	___of
___first	___fast
___then	___than
___on	___in
___far	___for

Fill in each space with one word from the three at the right:

1. He uses the ______________________ for his work. telephone / truck / tools

2. She uses it to talk to her ______________________. friends / relatives / people

3. Local calls do not ______________________ very much. happen / take / cost

4. Long distance ______________________ cost more money. letters / calls / presents

5. The Martines ______________________ their telephone. enjoy / miss / found

6. The ______________________ can offer assistance. boss / man / operator

7. Calls to people in the neighborhood are ______ calls. local / long distance / collect

8. Sometimes Mr. Martine calls his ______________________. dentist / florist / relatives

9. Each ______________________ has an area code. call / number / book

10. Local calls are ______________________ to dial. hard / easy / smooth

Write the missing words in the spaces:

TODAY	YESTERDAY
________________	made
________________	asked
________________	enjoyed
________________	dialed
________________	knew
________________	was
________________	lived
________________	telephoned
________________	did
________________	were
________________	used
________________	needed
________________	had

Write the missing words in the spaces:

ONE	MORE THAN ONE
home	______________
telephone	______________
dial	______________
wife	______________
friend	______________
person	______________
relative	______________
city	______________
area code	______________
number	______________
operator	______________
call	______________
neighborhood	______________

Put a circle around a smaller word in each of these words. Follow example:

has	friends
uses	calls
sometimes	neighborhood
another	not
distance	this
know	call
then	calling
his	than
asks	and
their	assistance
asking	without

Arrange the letters to make words:

m e h o ______________	b u m e r n ______________
r o k w ______________	e c a n s t i d ______________
n e t l e p o e h ______________	p l e h ______________
i a d l ______________	t o r o p e r a ______________
s o c t ______________	n a t c e s s a i s ______________
h e t o n a r ______________	y o n e j ______________
d e c o ______________	t i h w o u t ______________
r a e a ______________	

Use each of these words in a sentence:

1. telephone ______________________________.
2. local ______________________________.
3. dial ______________________________.
4. another ______________________________.
5. long distance ______________________________.
6. area code ______________________________.
7. expensive ______________________________.
8. operator ______________________________.
9. assistance ______________________________.
10. cost ______________________________.
11. without ______________________________.
12. help ______________________________.

Fill in the missing words:

Mr. Martine has a ____________ in his home. He needs it for his ________. His _______ uses it to talk to her _______.

Telephone calls to people in the __________ are ______ calls. Local _______ are easy to _______ and do not ______ very much.

Sometimes Mr. Martine ___________ his _______ who live in another ________. This is a long ________ telephone ______. He needs to know the area ______ of the city he is calling as well as the telephone _________ of his relatives. Mr. Martine ______ the ______ code first (503) and then he ______ the telephone number (124-5687).

Long _________ calls are more _________ than _______ telephone calls. If Mr. Martine needs _______ in using his _______ he ______ the operator and asks for ____________.

Mr. and Mrs. Martine _____ their telephone. They know how to make ______ and long _______ telephone ______ without _________ the _______ for ____________.

Enjoy doing this crossword puzzle:

DOWN

1. Space.
2. Speaking on the ________.
3. Going a long ________.
4. How much did your coat ______.
7. What is your telephone ______.

ACROSS

4. Use the area ________.
6. Help.
8. ________ the telephone number.
9. Ask the ________ for assistance.

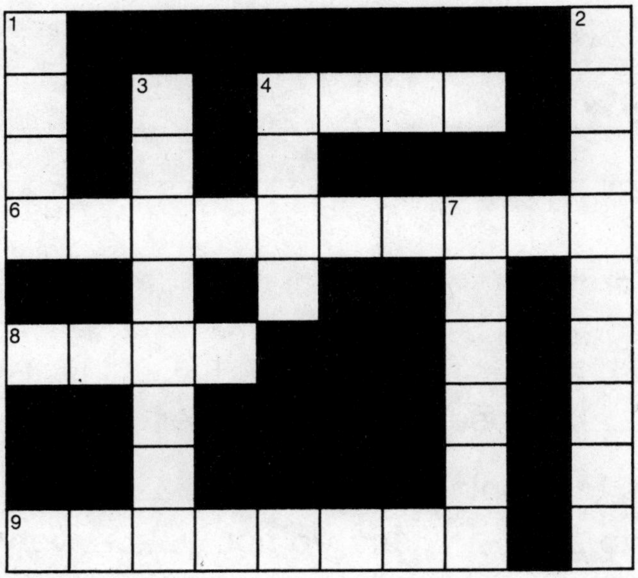

1
2
3
4
6
7
8
9

MIAMI, FL. 33132
DETROIT, MI. 48202
ATLANTA, GA. 30303
HONOLULU, HI. 96813
CHICAGO, IL. 60628
LOS ANGELES, CA. 92012
NEW YORK, N.Y. 10002

What Is Your Zip Code?

When you address a postcard or a letter, you need to know the zip code as well as the exact address of the person to whom you are writing.

Every mail address has a zip code. Do you know your zip code? Have you made sure that your friends and relatives know it?

The post office has worked out a number called a zip code for every city and place in the country. Every post office has a list of all the zip code numbers anywhere in the country. If you don't know the zip code of the person or business to which you are writing, the post office will be glad to give it to you.

The zip code number helps the post office employees to sort the mail and make sure it is delivered as quickly as possible. Mail without a zip code is delayed until the post office employees have time to look it up.

Check the words that are in the story "What Is Your Zip Code?":

___write	___wrote
___know	___knew
___well	___wall
___person	___parson
___give	___gave
___sure	___sore
___it	___at
___zip	___zap
___for	___far
___country	___county
___list	___last
___letter	___litter
___post	___past
___make	___mike
___have	___hive
___time	___tame

Arrange the letters to make words:

p i z d e c o ______________	l a y e d e d ______________
r e d a d s s ______________	k e m a ______________
d r e n i f s ______________	r y t o n u c ______________
t a l i r e s e v ______________	s s n i e b u s ______________
b r u m n e ______________	t r i w i n g ______________
c e l p a ______________	l i c u k y q ______________
l s i t ______________	l o m e y s e e p ______________

Write the correct words in the spaces:

ONE	MORE THAN ONE
zip code	____________
postcard	____________
letter	____________
address	____________
person	____________
friend	____________
relative	____________
number	____________
city	____________
place	____________
country	____________
business	____________
post office	____________
employee	____________

Write the correct words in the spaces:

TODAY	YESTERDAY
____________	was
____________	wrote
____________	needed
____________	knew
____________	had
____________	did
____________	made
____________	worked
____________	called
____________	gave
____________	helped
____________	sorted
____________	delivered
____________	delayed

Write these words in the spaces:

postcard

person

number

business

place

without

possible

writing

anywhere

mail

address

post office

zip code

Fill in the missing words in these sentences:

When you address a ________________ or a ____________, you need to know the ________________ as well as the exact __________ of the ___________ to whom you are writing.

Every mail ____________ has a zip ________. Do you know your __________ code? Have you made ________ that your ____________ and ____________ know it?

The ________________ has worked out a ____________ called a zip _________ for every city and ___________ in the ___________. Every post office has a _________ of all the zip code numbers anywhere in the country. If you don't know the _______ code of the ________ or business to which you are ____________, the post office will be _______ to give it to you.

The zip code __________ helps the post office ___________ to sort the ____________ and make sure it is ____________ as quickly as ______________. Mail _____________ a zip code is ____________ until the post office ______________ have time to look it up.

Enjoy doing this crossword puzzle:

DOWN

1. Make every __________ effort.
2. Slow down.
3. A picture __________.
4. Assistance.

ACROSS

1. One man or woman.
3. Where a package is mailed. (two words)
5. A worker.
6. A package is __________ to me.

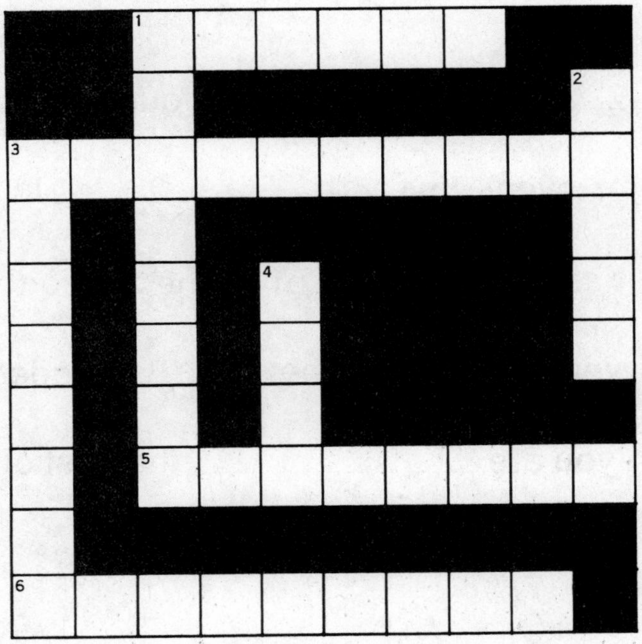
1
2
3
4
5
6

Mrs. L. Simmons
1903 Lake Ave.
Rochester, N.Y. 14620
PLACE
FIRST
CLASS
STAMP
HERE
Mr. Jack Simmons
216 Main Street
Syracuse, New York
13203

Jack Left His Sweater At My House

My nephew Jack left his sweater at my house. He lives in another city and can't come back to get it for a long time. I wrote a letter to him to tell him that I would mail the sweater to him.

First I addressed an envelope. I wrote Jack's full name. Next, I wrote the number of his house and the name of the street. Then I wrote the name of his city and state with his zip code number.

At the top left-hand corner of the envelope, I put my name and full address. I made sure to include my zip code number.

On a sheet of paper I wrote:

___________ 14, 198_

Dear Jack,

I am sending the sweater you left at my house so you can wear it to work. I put it in a box and will mail it at the post office today.

Love,
Lydia

Check the words that are in the story "Jack Left His Sweater At My House":

___lift	___left
___lives	___loves
___back	___buck
___get	___got
___far	___for
___long	___lung
___tame	___time
___Jack	___Jock
___till	___tell
___ham	___him
___sand	___send
___his	___has
___fast	___first
___full	___fill
___his	___has
___wrote	___write
___than	___then
___top	___tap
___put	___pit
___sure	___sore
___at	___it
___will	___wall
___past	___post
___love	___live

Arrange the letters to make words:

s d r s e a d ____________________

p r a p e ____________________

s n e d n i g ____________________

x o b ____________________

l i a m ____________________

t a y o d ____________________

d l e i n u c ____________________

t e x n ____________________

p h e n e w ____________________

t r e s e a w ____________________

Write the correct words in the spaces:

ONE	MORE THAN ONE
____________	envelopes
____________	nephews
____________	houses
____________	cities
____________	post offices
____________	boxes
____________	states
____________	names
____________	numbers
____________	streets
____________	corners

Put a circle around a smaller word in each of these words. Follow example:

(live)s	made
his	dear
sweater	mailing
another	can
letter	mail
send	office
addressed	today
then	box
corner	

Write the correct words in the spaces:

NOW	**YESTERDAY**
leave	________________
mail	________________
put	________________
live	________________
come	________________
wear	________________
send	________________
address	________________
write	________________
make	________________
include	________________

Use each of these words in a sentence:

1. sweater ____.
2. nephew ____.
3. another ____.
4. first ____.
5. envelope ____.
6. next ____.
7. number ____.
8. name ____.
9. street ____.
10. left-hand corner ____.
11. include ____.
12. zip code ____.
13. sheet ____.
14. paper ____.
15. left ____.
16. wear ____.
17. work ____.
18. box ____.
19. mail ____.
20. today ____.

Write these words in the spaces:

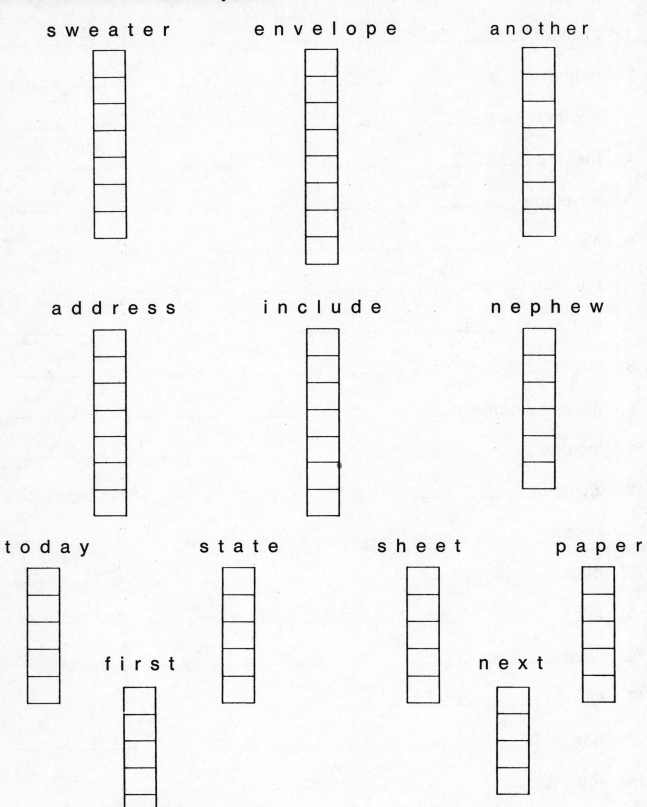

sweater

envelope

another

address

include

nephew

today

state

sheet

paper

first

next

Fill in the missing words:

My ______________ Jack left his ______________ at my house. He lives in ______________ city and can't come back to get it for a long ______________. I ______________ a ______________ to him to tell him that I would ______________ the ______________ to him.

First I ______________ an envelope. I ______________ Jack's full ______________. Next, I wrote the ______________ of his ______________ and the name of the street. Then I wrote the name of his ______________ and ______________ with his ______________ number. At the top ______________ corner of the ______________ I put my name and ______________ address. I made sure to ______________ my zip code number.

On a sheet of ______________ I wrote:

______________, 198__

______________,

I am ______________ the ______________ you left at my ______________ so you can ______________ it to ______________. I put it in a ______________ and will ______________ it at the post office ______________.

______________,

Lydia

Enjoy doing this crossword puzzle:

DOWN

1. Jack left his__________at my house.
2. My nephew's__________is Jack.
4. Jack__________his sweater at my house.

ACROSS

2. Your sister's son.
3. What the post office delivers.
5. One piece of paper.

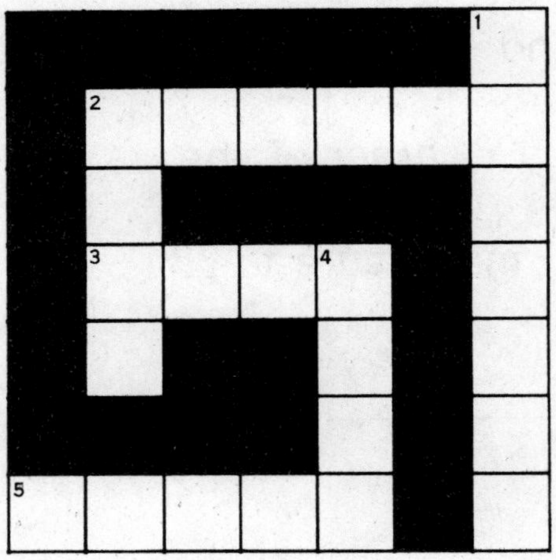

1
2
3
4
5

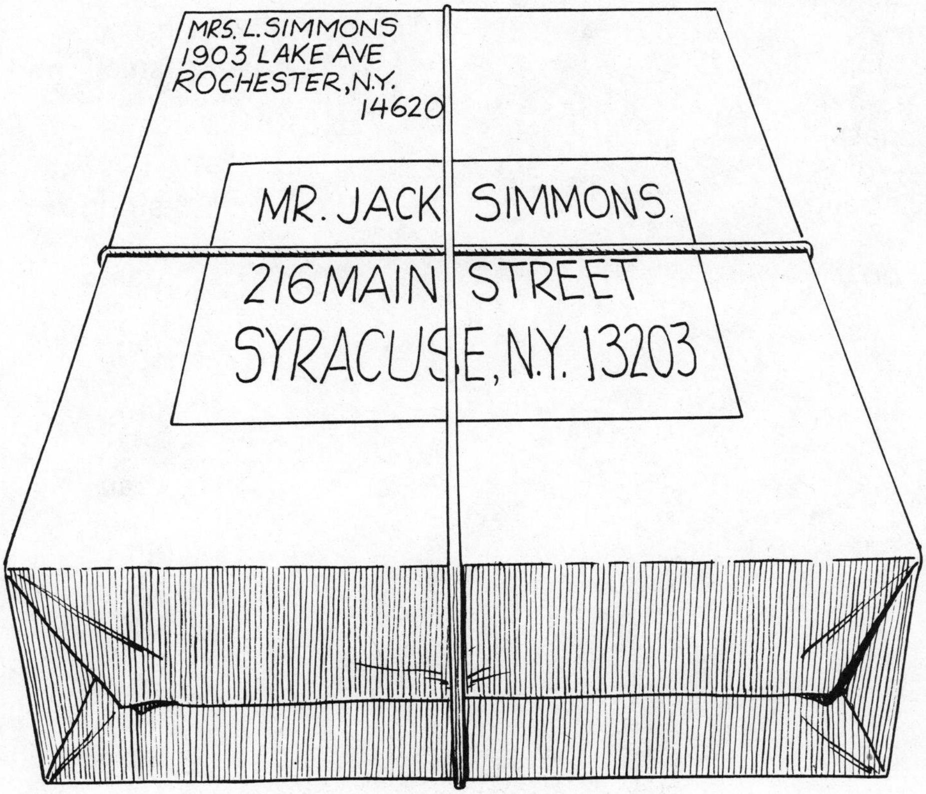
MRS. L. SIMMONS
1903 LAKE AVE
ROCHESTER, N.Y.
14620
MR. JACK SIMMONS.
216 MAIN STREET
SYRACUSE, N.Y. 13203

Lydia Sends Jack His Sweater

Lydia put Jack's sweater into a small box. Then she wrapped the box in brown wrapping paper and tied the package with strong string. She did not fasten the ends of the package with scotch tape because she knew the post office would charge first class letter postage if it was sealed. When the ends of a package are not sealed the postage is much cheaper.

Then Lydia took a label and carefully wrote Jack's full name and address with the zip code number. She wrote very legibly so the name and address could be easily read and the package delivered quickly.

On the top left-hand corner, Lydia wrote her name, address and zip code. Then she took the package to the post office near her house and mailed it at the package window.

Check the words that are in the story "Lydia Sends Jack His Sweater":

___sends	___sands
___small	___smell
___pat	___put
___strong	___string
___post	___past
___tape	___type
___letter	___litter
___then	___than
___full	___fill
___top	___tip
___wrapped	___trapped
___left	___lift

Arrange the letters to make words:

l a e s d e ____________________

e d t i ____________________

e d r a ____________________

l e d i a m ____________________

r a c h e p e ____________________

g l i b y e l ____________________

k o t o ____________________

p a d r e w p ____________________

t e d e f a s n ____________________

Write the correct words in the spaces:

TODAY	YESTERDAY
____________	put
____________	wrapped
____________	tied
____________	fastened
____________	knew
____________	charged
____________	sealed
____________	were
____________	took
____________	wrote
____________	read
____________	delivered
____________	mailed

Write the correct words in the spaces:

ONE	MORE THAN ONE
box	____________
paper	____________
package	____________
string	____________
end	____________
tape	____________
letter	____________
label	____________
name	____________
address	____________
corner	____________
number	____________
home	____________
window	____________

Write these words in the spaces:

s w e a t e r

w r a p p i n g p a p e r

f a s t e n

p o s t a g e

s e a l e d

c h e a p e r

l a b e l

c a r e f u l l y

l e g i b l y

d e l i v e r e d

w i n d o w

Use each of these words in a sentence:

1. sweater ______________________________.
2. wrap ______________________________.
3. string ______________________________.
4. label ______________________________.
5. package ______________________________.
6. carefully ______________________________.
7. legibly ______________________________.
8. corner ______________________________.
9. deliver ______________________________.
10. easily ______________________________.
11. quickly ______________________________.
12. box ______________________________.
13. wrapping paper ______________________________.
14. tied ______________________________.
15. fasten ______________________________.
16. scotch tape ______________________________.
17. strong ______________________________.
18. sealed ______________________________.
19. cheap ______________________________.
20. zip code ______________________________.

Fill in the missing words:

Lydia put Jack's ________________ into a small ____________. Then she ________________ the box in brown ________________ paper and ____________ the ______________ with strong ___________. She did not ______________ the ends of the __________________ with scotch _________ because she knew the post ____________ would _________ first class letter ______________ if it was ________________. When the ________________ of a package are not ________________ the postage is much ________________.

Then Lydia took a ____________ and ______________ wrote Jack's _________ name and address with the zip ____________ number. She wrote very ________________ so the name and ____________ could be __________ read, and the __________ delivered ______________.

On the top _____________ corner, Lydia wrote her name, __________ and zip code. Then she took the ______________ to the ______________ office near her house and ___________ it at the package ______________.

Enjoy doing this crossword puzzle:

DOWN

1. Lydia wrapped the package ____________________.
2. ____________________ code.
3. Lydia put the address on the ____________________.
4. ______________ stamps.

ACROSS

1. Zip ________________.
5. Lydia did not ______________ the ends.
6. She wrote ________________ so the mailman could read.

Word Practice

These are new words in the stories you have read. Check the words you remember:

___try
___good
___parsley
___pieces
___salt
___mixture
___soup
___saucepan
___four
___serve
___put
___recipe

___drop
___Friday
___tarragon
___boil
___condensed soup
___creamed
___watch
___large

___postcard
___letter
___zip code
___exact
___address
___every
___relatives
___list
___business
___quickly
___employees
___delivered
___possible
___delayed

___sweater
___nephew
___first
___envelope
___next
___number
___same
___street
___left-hand corner
___include
___sheet
___paper
___wear
___mail

___wrapping paper
___fasten
___postage
___sealed
___cheaper
___label
___carefully
___legibly
___window

___telephone
___local
___dial
___another
___long distance
___area code
___expensive
___operator
___assistance
___cost
___without
___help

Use the spaces below to write in alphabetical order the words from the previous page:

a

b

c

d

e

f

g

h

i

l

m

n

o

p

q

r

s

t

w

z

EXIT
OUT
AB
WHEAT
flakes

The Checkout Counter

Sarah Lake works in a large supermarket. She works at the checkout counter. There are six other food checkers in the supermarket. They are all good friends and like to work together.

At first, Sarah was bewildered by the many kinds of foods, the many aisles, and the frozen food cases with the many hundreds of food items. Many of the food items were new and strange to Sarah, but she quickly learned the names of the new foods and even tried some of them at home.

Each day Sarah checked the purchases of many customers. She rang up the price of each item on the register and told the customers the amount of money they owed. Then she took the money and gave the customers a receipt and any change.

Sarah works five days a week and makes good money. Some days the hours seem long, and she is very tired at the end of the day. But Sarah enjoys her work at the checkout counter in the supermarket. She has worked there for three years and has a responsible job.

Check the words that are in the story "The Checkout Counter":

___sex	___six
___food	___feed
___ill	___all
___it	___at
___now	___new
___end	___and
___even	___oven
___some	___same
___chucked	___checked
___rang	___rung
___many	___money
___then	___than
___gave	___give
___lung	___long

Put a circle around a smaller word in each of these words. Follow example:

super(market)	years
checkout	together
counter	many
strange	bewildered
learned	name
them	some
checked	rang
purchases	price
customers	told
owed	amount

Fill in each space with one word from the three at the right:

1. Sarah works in a large ________________. — factory / supermarket / office
2. At first Sarah was ________________. — bewildered / late / tired
3. She rang up the price of each ____________. — book / sale / item
4. She works ________________ days a week. — three / four / five
5. She has a ________________ job. — hard / responsible / big

Write the correct words in the spaces:

TODAY	YESTERDAY
________	worked
are	________
like	________
________	bewildered
learn	________
________	tried
check	________
ring	________
tell	________
________	owed
take	________
________	gave
________	made
________	seemed
is	________
enjoy	________
________	had

Write the correct words in the spaces:

ONE	MORE THAN ONE
________	supermarkets
counter	________
________	checkers
friend	________
________	kinds
________	foods
aisle	________

ONE	**MORE THAN ONE**
case	______________
hundred	______________
______________	items
______________	names
home	______________
______________	days
customer	______________
______________	prices
______________	registers
receipt	______________
______________	jobs
week	______________
______________	hours
year	______________

Arrange the letters to make words:

g e n r a t s ______________

l a e i s s ______________

z e n o r f ______________

t r e s i g r e ______________

r e d i t ______________

p r e c e i t ______________

t r a k r e m u e p s ______________

x s i ______________

g e c h a n ______________

t h e r g o t e ______________

Use each of these words in a sentence:

1. supermarket ____.
2. checkout counter ____.
3. six ____.
4. together ____.
5. bewildered ____.
6. aisles ____.
7. frozen ____.
8. cases ____.
9. hundreds ____.
10. items ____.
11. strange ____.
12. purchases ____.
13. customers ____.
14. register ____.
15. receipt ____.
16. change ____.
17. tired ____.
18. responsible ____.

Fill in the missing words:

Sarah Lake works in a large ______________. She works at the check-out ____________. There are ______ other food ______________ in the supermarket. They are all good _________ and like to work __________.

At first, Sarah was ______________ by the many kinds of foods, the many _________, and the ________ food cases with many _________ of food items. Many of the food ___________ were new and ___________ to Sarah, but she quickly learned the names of the new ________ and even tried some of them at _________.

Each day Sarah checked the ____________ of many ___________. She rang up the _________ of each item on the ________ and told the customers the _________ of money they owed. Then she took the money and gave the customers a __________ and any __________.

Sarah works five days a _________ and makes good __________. Some days the hours seem long, and she is very _________ at the end of the day. But Sarah _________ her work at the __________ counter in the _________. She has worked there for three years and has a ____________ job.

Can You Tell Me?

"Can you tell me where to find a drugstore?" Beulah stopped walking. A woman coming along the street had asked her the question.

"Oh, yes, I can," she said. "I just came from there. It is only two blocks from here."

"Please tell me how to find it," said the woman. "I live on the other side of the city. I'm a stranger in this neighborhood."

Beulah pointed and said, "Go to the corner. Then turn to the right. Walk two blocks and you will see the drugstore on the corner. It's a large store with a big sign. You can't miss it."

"Thank you very much," said the woman and hurried to the corner.

Beulah watched until the woman reached the corner and turned in the right direction. Then she went on her way home.

Put a circle around a smaller word in each of these words.
Follow example:

(stop)ped	neighborhood
woman	pointed
walking	corner
along	watched
had	reached
asked	turned
there	direction
blocks	please
stranger	

Arrange the letters to make words:

s b l o c k ____________________

r a n g r e t s ____________________

t e d n o i p ____________________

h a n k t ____________________

c r r e n o ____________________

t h r i g ____________________

e d u r n t ____________________

m a n o w ____________________

l e p e s a ____________________

s n i g ____________________

Write the correct words in the spaces:

TODAY	YESTERDAY
______________	told
find	______________
walk	______________
______________	came
______________	asked
say	______________
______________	was
live	______________
point	______________
go	______________
______________	turned
see	______________
______________	missed
______________	hurried
______________	watched
reach	______________

Write the missing words in the spaces:

ONE	MORE THAN ONE
______________	drugstores
woman	______________
______________	streets
______________	questions
block	______________
city	______________
stranger	______________
______________	neighborhoods
way	______________
______________	corners
______________	signs
______________	directions
home	______________

Check the words that are in the story "Can you Tell Me?":

___tell	___drag
___find	___women
___step	___drug
___muss	___with
___miss	___turn
___watch	___live
___then	___woman
___stop	___love
___than	___torn
___tall	___fund

Use each of these words in a sentence:

1. blocks ______________________________.
2. drugstore ______________________________.
3. pointed ______________________________.
4. reached ______________________________.
5. stranger ______________________________.
6. watch ______________________________.
7. hurried ______________________________.
8. question ______________________________.
9. watched ______________________________.
10. hurry ______________________________.
11. neighborhood ______________________________.
12. direction ______________________________.
13. please ______________________________.
14. miss ______________________________.
15. neighborhoods ______________________________.
16. sign ______________________________.
17. home ______________________________.
18. other ______________________________.
19. corner ______________________________.
20. walked ______________________________.

Fill in the missing words:

"Can you tell me where to find a ____________?" Beulah stopped ____________. A woman coming along the ____________ had asked her the ____________.

"Oh, yes, I can," she ____________. "I just ____________ from there. It is only two ____________ from here."

"____________ tell me how to find it," said the woman. "I live on the other ____________ of the ____________. I'm a ____________ in this ____________."

Beulah ____________ and said, "Go to the ____________. Then turn to the ____________. Walk two ____________ and you will see the drugstore on the ____________. It's a large store with a big ____________. You can't ____________ it."

"____________ you very much," said the woman and ____________ to the ____________.

Beulah ____________ until the woman ____________ the corner and turned in the right ____________. Then she went on her way home.

SOCIAL SECURITY ACT
ACCOUNT NUMBER
162-24-5405
HAS BEEN
ESTABLISHED FOR
MARTIN E. J. ROBINS
Martin E. J. Robins
WORKER'S SIGNATURE

Marty Lost His Social Security Card

Marty lost his Social Security card. He went to the Social Security office near where he lived.

"I've lost my Social Security card. Can I get another card?" he asked the man at the desk.

"Oh, yes. Don't worry," was the answer. "This is what you must do. Here is an application blank. Fill in all of the items. If you need help in answering any of the items I will be glad to help you."

Marty filled in the answers to all of the items on the blank. When he was finished be gave the blank to the man at the desk.

"I will send this to our main office," said the man. "In a few days you will receive a new card in the mail. Keep it safe."

"Thank you," said Marty. "I was afraid I was in trouble and wouldn't be able to work any more."

"Oh, no," said the man. "It will be O.K. Try not to lose the new card. Keep it in a safe place."

Check the words that are in the story "Marty Lost His Social Security Card":

___cord	___card
___lived	___loved
___want	___went
___last	___lost
___got	___get
___men	___man
___it	___at
___as	___is
___must	___mist
___fall	___fill
___on	___in
___if	___of
___well	___will
___bank	___blank
___gave	___give
___men	___man
___sand	___send
___mare	___more
___now	___new

Write the correct words in the spaces:

TODAY	YESTERDAY
lose	________________
live	________________
get	________________
ask	________________
finish	________________
is	________________
________________	filled
________________	did
need	________________
________________	tried
________________	gave
________________	sent
am	________________
receive	________________
________________	kept
________________	worked
say	________________

Write the missing words in the spaces:

ONE	MORE THAN ONE
blank	________________
________________	items
________________	answers
________________	men

day
____
desk
____
____
place

____
cards
____
offices
troubles
____

Arrange the letters to make words:

s t o l ______________

d r a c ______________

r e n a ______________

o r a t h e n ______________

y r o w r ______________

k l a b n ______________

p l e h ______________

s n i f e d i h ______________

e f o i f c ______________

d r a a i f ______________

b e u l o r t ______________

s e l o ______________

e p k e ______________

f e s a ______________

Put a circle around a smaller word in each of these words.
Follow example:

office
where
another
asked
man
answer
this
items
any
filled
when

lived
card
days
place
what
here
fill
glad
hear
thank
not

Use each of these words in a sentence:

1. lost ______________________________.
2. Social Security card ______________________________.
3. near ______________________________.
4. another ______________________________.
5. worry ______________________________.
6. application ______________________________.
7. items ______________________________.
8. answering ______________________________.
9. glad ______________________________.
10. help ______________________________.
11. blank ______________________________.
12. finished ______________________________.
13. desk ______________________________.
14. main office ______________________________.
15. received ______________________________.
16. safe ______________________________.
17. afraid ______________________________.
18. trouble ______________________________.
19. lose ______________________________.
20. place ______________________________.

Fill in the missing words:

Marty ________ his Social ______________ card. He went to the ____________Security office near where he ________.

"I've lost my Social Security _______. Can I get ______________ card?" he asked the man at the ___________.

"Oh, yes. Don't ___________," was the __________. "This is what you must ________. Here is an application ________. Fill in all of the __________. If you need help in ________________ any of the items I will be ________ to ___________ you."

Marty filled in the ____________ to all of the __________ on the __________. When he was finished he gave the ________ to the man at the desk.

"I will send this to our main __________," said the man. "In a few _______ you will ___________ a new card in the __________. Keep it ________."

"Thank you," said Marty. "I was ________ I was in ________ and wouldn't be able to __________ any more."

"Oh, no," said the man. "It will be O.K. Try not to _______ the new __________. Keep it in a safe ___________."

BEST OF OUR
NAVY BEATS
WEST POINT

A Sudden Downpour

Yesterday there was a sudden downpour at about five o'clock in the afternoon. No one expected it to rain yesterday. The newspaper forecast and the TV weathermen had said it would be sunny and clear all day.

Many people were caught in the heavy rain just as they were going home from work. Some people waited in doorways hoping the rain would stop soon. Others ran through the rain. They did not mind getting wet as it was a very hot day. There was no thunder or lightning, but lots of rain, rain, rain.

In about fifteen or twenty minutes, the rain stopped as suddenly as it had begun, and the sky cleared. It was only a shower, but a great deal of rain fell.

That night the weatherman on TV said that nearly half an inch of rain had fallen during the sudden downpour that afternoon. He reported that many people were delayed getting home on account of the shower, and there were many traffic tie-ups because of it. However, the weatherman promised cool weather for that night and a clear and sunny sky for the following day.

Check the words that are in the story "A Sudden Downpour":

___it	___at
___on	___in
___end	___and
___wore	___were
___ruin	___rain
___same	___some
___step	___stop
___ran	___run
___not	___net
___hat	___hot
___stepped	___stopped
___began	___begun
___but	___bat
___fall	___fell
___hid	___had
___fur	___for

Fill in each space with one word from the three at the right:

1.	Yesterday there was a sudden __________________.	storm flood downpour
2.	No one expected it to __________________.	rain snow freeze
3.	It was supposed to be __________________ all day.	cold sunny foggy
4.	Many people were __________________ in the rain.	singing dancing caught
5.	Some people waited in __________________.	doorways buses airplanes
6.	Others did not mind getting __________________.	dry wet home
7.	The rain stopped __________________.	soon suddenly later
8.	Nearly half an inch of __________________ had fallen.	snow rain dust
9.	There were __________________ traffic tie-ups.	some no many
10.	The weatherman promised a __________________ sky.	dark cloudy sunny

Write the correct words in the spaces:

TODAY	YESTERDAY
______________	expected
______________	rained
say	______________
is	______________
are	______________
______________	caught
stop	______________
______________	ran
mind	______________
______________	waited
clear	______________
fall	______________
report	______________
______________	delayed
______________	promised

Write the correct words in the spaces:

ONE	MORE THAN ONE
afternoon	______________
______________	downpours
newspaper	______________
______________	days
person	______________
______________	homes
doorway	______________

minute

____

shower

____

inch

____

____

skies

____

weathermen

____

nights

Put a circle around a smaller word in each of these words. Follow example:

yester(day)	there
o'clock	downpour
afternoon	expected
said	had
clear	sunny
they	many
waited	going
stop	doorways
not	ran
was	others
lightning	thunder
twenty	stopped
suddenly	begun
cleared	shower
great	that
weatherman	nearly
inch	fallen
reported	delayed
getting	however
promised	following

Use each of these words in a sentence:

1. downpour ______________________________.
2. afternoon ______________________________.
3. expected ______________________________.
4. rain ______________________________.
5. sunny ______________________________.
6. clear ______________________________.
7. caught ______________________________.
8. doorways ______________________________.
9. thunder ______________________________.
10. lightning ______________________________.
11. shower ______________________________.
12. sudden ______________________________.
13. weatherman ______________________________.
14. traffic ______________________________.
15. following ______________________________.

Fill in the missing words:

Yesterday there was a sudden ______________ at about five ______________ in the afternoon. No one ______________ it to rain ______________. The ______________ forecast and the TV weathermen had said it would be ______________ and clear all ______________.

Many ______________ were caught in the ______________ rain just as they were going home from work. Some people ______________ in ______________ hoping the ______________ would stop ______________. Others ran ______________ the rain. They did not ______________ getting ______________ as it was a very hot ______________. There was no ______________ or ______________, but lots of rain, ______________, rain.

In about ______________ or twenty __________, the rain stopped as ______________ as it had begun, and the sky ______________. It was only a ___________, but a great deal of rain fell.

That night the ____________________ on TV said that nearly half an ___________ of rain had fallen during the sudden ______________ that ____________. He __________ that many people were ___________ getting home on ____________ of the ___________, and there were many traffic _____________ because of it. However, the weatherman promised cool ____________ for that night and a __________ and ___________ sky for the following day.

Arrange the letters to make words:

p o u r n w o d ________________ s e n l y u d d ________________

t e r a f o n o n ________________ e y l a d ________________

n u s n y ________________ d e y a l e d ________________

a i n r ________________ c i f f a r t ________________

n e r d u t h ________________ l o o c ________________

w o l l i n g o f ________________

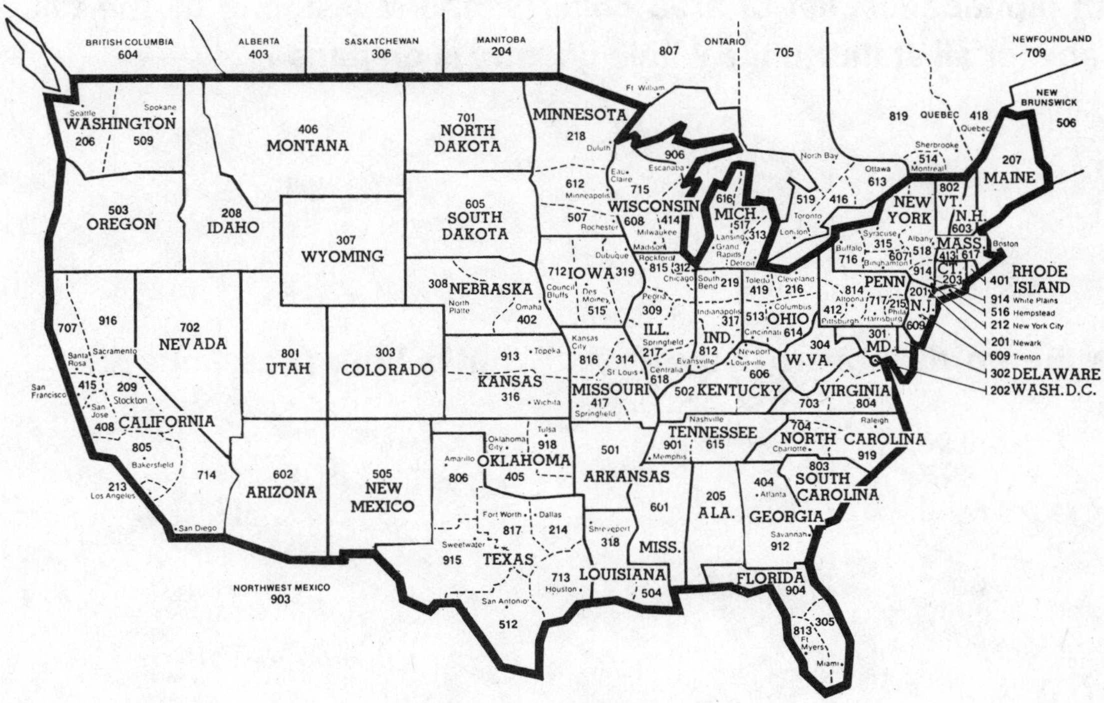
BRITISH COLUMBIA 604
ALBERTA 403
SASKATCHEWAN 306
MANITOBA 204
807
ONTARIO
705
NEWFOUNDLAND 709
NEW BRUNSWICK
506
819 QUEBEC 418
Quebec
Sherbrooke
514 Montreal
Ottawa 613
North Bay
519 416
Toronto
London
Ft William
WASHINGTON
Seattle
Spokane
206 509
406 MONTANA
701 NORTH DAKOTA
MINNESOTA 218
Duluth
612 Minneapolis
507 Rochester
503 OREGON
208 IDAHO
307 WYOMING
605 SOUTH DAKOTA
308 NEBRASKA
North Platte
Omaha 402
712 IOWA 319
Council Bluffs
Des Moines 515
Dubuque
WISCONSIN
Eau Claire
715
608 414
Milwaukee
Madison
906
Escanaba
MICH.
616
517
313
Lansing
Grand Rapids
Detroit
Rockford
815 312
Chicago
South Bend 219
Toledo 419
Cleveland 216
Columbus
513 OHIO 614
Cincinnati
Indianapolis 317
IND. 812
Peoria 309
ILL.
Springfield 217
Centralia 618
St Louis
Evansville
Newport
Louisville
606
502 KENTUCKY
707 916
Santa Rosa
Sacramento
San Francisco
415 209
San Jose
Stockton
408 CALIFORNIA
805
Bakersfield
213
Los Angeles
San Diego
714
702 NEVADA
801 UTAH
303 COLORADO
913 Topeka
KANSAS 316 Wichita
Kansas City
816 314
MISSOURI
417 Springfield
602 ARIZONA
505 NEW MEXICO
Amarillo 806
Oklahoma City
Tulsa 918
OKLAHOMA 405
Fort Worth 817
Dallas 214
Sweetwater 915
TEXAS
713 Houston
San Antonio
512
NORTHWEST MEXICO 903
501 ARKANSAS
Shreveport 318
LOUISIANA 504
601 MISS.
Nashville
TENNESSEE 901 615
Memphis
205 ALA.
404 Atlanta
GEORGIA
Savannah 912
FLORIDA 904
305
813 Ft Myers
Miami
704 NORTH CAROLINA
Charlotte
Raleigh
919
803 SOUTH CAROLINA
VIRGINIA 703 804
304 W.VA.
301 MD.
PENN
814 Altoona
717 215
412 Pittsburgh
Harrisburg
Phila
NEW YORK
Buffalo 716
Syracuse 315
Binghamton
607
Albany 518
914
201
N.J.
609
802 VT.
N.H. 603
MASS. 413 617
Boston
CT. 203
207 MAINE
401 RHODE ISLAND
914 White Plains
516 Hempstead
212 New York City
201 Newark
609 Trenton
302 DELAWARE
202 WASH.D.C.

What Is Your Area Code?

If you have a telephone, you also have an area code number. The area code number is printed on your telephone with the telephone number. Area code numbers are used only when making long distance telephone calls.

The telephone company has worked out a number for every state or area in the country. If you live in the state of California in Hollywood, Los Angeles, Glendale, Beverly Hills or Burbank, your area code is 213. But if you live in Stockton, California, your area code is 209. If you live anywhere in the state of Maine, your area code is 207. In the state of Alabama, all places have 205 for the area code. In the state of Connecticut, all places have 203 for the area code.

If you live in New York City, your area code is 212. In another part of the same state—in Dunkirk, Lockport, Niagara Falls, Olean, Rochester, Tonawanda, or Buffalo—the area code is 716. The area code for Mexico is 903, and the area code is 809 for Puerto Rico and the Virgin Islands.

An alphabetical list of area code numbers assigned by the telephone company for all states in the whole country is on page 72.

Check the words that are in the story "What Is Your Area Code?":

___have	___live
___of	___if
___on	___an
___is	___as
___lung	___long
___tells	___calls
___for	___far
___in	___on
___county	___country
___love	___live
___port	___part
___some	___same
___lost	___list
___list	___last
___ill	___all
___whole	___while

Fill in each space with one word from the three at the right:

1. Each __________ number has an area code.	apartment street telephone
2. It is printed on your __________.	telephone book door
3. Maine's __________ code is 207.	secret area zip
4. Alabama has only one area __________.	code left together
5. Some __________ have several area codes.	cities states towns
6. Area codes are for long distance __________.	jumps trips calls
7. The area code for __________ is 903.	Alabama Mexico Puerto Rico
8. The telephone __________ worked out the numbers.	man company operator
9. The area code for __________ is 213.	Hollywood Maine New York
10. __________ has only one area code.	Texas Alabama Florida

Write the correct words in the spaces:

TODAY	YESTERDAY
have	________________
is	________________
________________	printed
are	________________
________________	assigned
________________	used
work	________________
________________	lived

Write the correct words in the spaces:

ONE	MORE THAN ONE
telephone	________________
number	________________
________________	codes
________________	telephone calls
________________	states
area	________________
________________	countries
place	________________
part	________________
list	________________

Put a circle around a smaller word in each of these words.
Follow example:

also
area
printed
only
when
call
country
Hollywood
Angeles
hills
another
same
islands
assigned

your
with
used
has
worked
for
Burbank
anywhere
places
Lockport
virgin
alphabetical
company

Arrange the letters to make words:

r i t e n p d ____________________

s e u d ____________________

l a c l ____________________

a t s t e ____________________

v e l i ____________________

c r y o n u t ____________________

c l a p e s ____________________

a p t r ____________________

h a n o t e r ____________________

l a c i t e b a h p l a ____________________

s d i a s g n e ____________________

n e o h p e l e t ____________________

Use each of these words in a sentence:

1. telephone ______________________________.
2. also ______________________________.
3. printed ______________________________.
4. company ______________________________.
5. state ______________________________.
6. country ______________________________.
7. California ______________________________.
8. anywhere ______________________________.
9. Maine ______________________________.
10. Alabama ______________________________.
11. Connecticut ______________________________.
12. whole ______________________________.
13. Mexico ______________________________.
14. assigned ______________________________.
15. Virgin Islands ______________________________.
16. alphabetical list ______________________________.

Fill in the missing words:

If you have a ____________, you also have an area ________ number. The ________ code __________ is ______________ on your telephone with the ________________ number. Area code ________________ are used only when making long ________________ telephone ____________.

The telephone ______________ has worked out a __________ for every ____________ or area in the ______________. If you ________ in the state of ______________ in Hollywood, ______________, Glendale, Beverly Hills or Burbank your area code is __________. But if you ______ in Stockton, California, your __________ code is ________. If you live ________ in the state of ________, your area code is 207. In the ________ of Alabama, all places have _______ for the area ______. In the state of _______________, all places have _______ for the area code.

If you live in New York City, your area code is ______. In ____________ part of the same state—in Dunkirk, Lockport, _______ Falls, Olean, ____________, Tonawanda, or __________—the area code is ________. The area code for Mexico is _____, and the area code is _____ for _______ Rico and the Virgin ______.

An ____________________ list of area code numbers ____________ by the telephone ________ for all states in the __________ country is on page ________.

Area Codes *Alphabetical list by States*

area code	location
ALABAMA	
205	All points
ALASKA	
907	All points
ARIZONA	
602	All points
ARKANSAS	
501	All points
CALIFORNIA	
805	Bakersfield
213	Beverly Hills
213	Burbank (L.A. County)
209	Fresno
213	Hollywood
213	Los Angeles
415	Oakland
415	Palo Alto
714	Pomona
916	Sacramento
714	San Diego
415	San Francisco
408	San Jose
415	San Mateo
707	Santa Rosa
209	Stockton
COLORADO	
303	All points
CONNECTICUT	
203	All points
DELAWARE	
302	All points
Dist. of COLUMBIA	
202	Washington, D.C.
FLORIDA	
813	Clearwater
904	Daytona Beach
305	Fort Lauderdale
813	Fort Meyers
305	Fort Pierce
904	Gainesville
305	Hialeah
904	Jacksonville
305	Key West
813	Lakeland
305	Miami
305	Orlando
904	Pensacola
305	Pompano Beach
813	Sarasota
904	Tallahassee
305	West Palm Beach
GEORGIA	
404	Athens
404	Atlanta
404	Augusta
404	Columbus
404	Gainesville
912	Macon
404	Marietta
404	Rome
912	Savannah
HAWAII	
808	All points
IDAHO	
208	All points
ILLINOIS	
618	Alton
312	Aurora
309	Bloomington
312	Chicago
217	Danville
217	Decatur
618	East St. Louis
312	Elgin
309	Galesburg
312	Highland Park
312	Hinsdale
815	Joliet
312	La Grange
309	Peoria
815	Rockford
217	Springfield
INDIANA	
219	Elkhart
812	Evansville
219	Gary
219	Hammond
317	Indianapolis
219	Michigan City
317	Muncie
219	South Bend
IOWA	
712	Council Bluffs
319	Davenport
515	Des Moines
KANSAS	
913	Salina
913	Topeka
316	Wichita
KENTUCKY	
606	Ashland
502	Frankfort
502	Louisville
LOUISIANA	
504	Baton Rouge
504	New Orleans
318	Shreveport
MAINE	
207	All points
MARYLAND	
301	All points
MASSACHUSETTS	
413	Amherst
617	Attleboro
617	Barnstable
617	Boston
617	Brockton
617	Cambridge
617	Dedham
617	Fall River
617	Fitchburg
617	Framingham
617	Gardner
413	Greenfield
413	Holyoke
413	Longmeadow
617	Lowell
617	Lynn
617	Marblehead
617	New Bedford
413	North Adams
413	Northampton
413	Pittsfield
617	Quincy
617	Roxbury
413	Springfield
617	Taunton
617	Waltham
413	Westfield
617	Worcester
MICHIGAN	
313	Ann Arbor
616	Battle Creek
616	Benton Harbor
313	Dearborn
313	Detroit
313	Flint
616	Grand Rapids
517	Jackson
616	Kalamazoo
517	Lansing
906	Marquette
517	Midland
616	Niles
313	Pontiac
313	Port Huron
313	Royal Oak
517	Saginaw
616	St. Joseph
313	Wyandotte
MINNESOTA	
218	Duluth
612	Minneapolis
507	Rochester
612	St. Paul
MISSISSIPPI	
601	All points
MISSOURI	
314	Jefferson City
816	Kansas City
816	St. Joseph
314	St. Louis
417	Springfield
MONTANA	
406	All points
NEBRASKA	
402	Lincoln
308	North Platte
402	Omaha
NEVADA	
702	All points
NEW HAMPSHIRE	
603	All points
NEW JERSEY	
201	Asbury Park
609	Atlantic City
609	Barnegat
201	Bayonne
201	Bloomfield
201	Bound Brook
609	Bridgeton
609	Burlington
609	Camden
201	Carteret
201	Cliffside Park
201	Clifton
609	Collingswood
201	Dover
201	Eatontown
201	Elizabeth
201	Englewood
609	Ewing
201	Fair Lawn
201	Flemington
609	Fort Dix
201	Fort Lee
609	Glassboro
201	Glen Ridge
609	Gloucester
201	Hackensack
609	Haddonfield
201	Hasbrouck Hts
201	Hawthorne
201	Hoboken
201	Irvington
201	Jersey City
201	Kearny
201	Lakewood
201	Linden
201	Long Branch
201	Madison
201	Maplewood
201	Mendham
201	Metuchen
201	Millburn
201	Montclair
201	Morristown
609	Mount Holly
201	Newark
201	New Brunswick
201	Nutley
201	Orange
201	Paramus
201	Passaic
201	Paterson
201	Perth Amboy
201	Phillipsburg
201	Plainfield
609	Pleasantville
201	Point Pleasant
201	Pompton Lakes
609	Princeton
201	Red Bank
201	Ridgefield
201	Ridgewood
201	Rutherford
201	Somerville
201	South Amboy
201	Summit
201	Teaneck
609	Trenton
201	Union City
201	Verona
609	Vineland
201	Weehawken
201	Westfield
609	Wildwood
201	Woodbridge
609	Woodbury
201	Wyckoff
NEW MEXICO	
505	All points
NEW YORK	
518	Albany
516	Amagansett
516	Amityville
518	Amsterdam
914	Armonk Village
315	Auburn
516	Babylon
516	Baldwin
516	Bay Shore
914	Bedford Village
607	Binghamton
516	Brentwood
914	Brewster
516	Bridgehampton
914	Bronxville
516	Brookville
716	Buffalo
914	Callicoon
914	Carmel
516	Center Moriches
516	Central Islip
914	Chappaqua
518	Cohoes
914	Cold Spring (Putnam Co.)
516	Commack
914	Congers
607	Corning
607	Cortland
914	Croton-on-Hudson
516	Deer Park
914	Dobbs Ferry
716	Dunkirk
516	East Hampton
516	Eastport
914	Ellenville
607	Elmira
914	Elmsford
607	Endicott
914	Fallsburg
516	Farmingdale
516	Fire Island
516	Fishers Island
516	Freeport
315	Fulton
516	Garden City
914	Garrison
516	Glen Cove
518	Glens Falls
914	Grahamsville
516	Great Neck
914	Grossinger
315	Hamilton
516	Hampton Bays
914	Harrison
914	Hastings-on-Hudson
914	Haverstraw
516	Hempstead
518	Hudson
516	Huntington
914	Hurleyville
914	Irvington
516	Islip
607	Ithaca
914	Jeffersonville
914	Kerhonkson
914	Kiamesha
914	Kingston
914	Lake Huntington
914	Lakeland
516	Lake Success
914	Larchmont
914	Liberty
516	Lindenhurst
914	Livingston Manor
716	Lockport
516	Lynbrook
914	Mahopac
914	Mamaroneck
516	Manhasset
516	Massapequa
315	Massena
914	Middletown
516	Montauk Point
914	Monticello
914	Mt. Kisco
914	Mt. Vernon
914	Nanuet
914	Narrowsburg
315	Newark
914	Newburgh
914	New City
914	New Rochelle
212	New York City
716	Niagara Falls
607	Norwich
914	Nyack
716	Olean
315	Oneida
914	Ossining
315	Oswego
516	Oyster Bay
516	Patchogue
914	Pearl River
914	Peekskill
914	Pelham
914	Piermont
518	Plattsburgh
914	Pleasantville
914	Port Chester
516	Port Jefferson
516	Port Washington
315	Potsdam
914	Poughkeepsie
516	Riverhead
716	Rochester
516	Rockville Centre
315	Rome
516	Ronkonkoma
607	Roscoe
516	Roslyn
914	Rye
516	Sag Harbor
516	Sayville
914	Scarsdale
518	Schenectady
516	Shelter Island
914	Sloatsburg
516	Smithtown
516	Southampton
914	Spring Valley
914	Stony Point (Rockland Co.)
914	Suffern
315	Syracuse
914	Tarrytown
518	Ticonderoga
716	Tonawanda
518	Troy
914	Tuckahoe
315	Utica
516	Valley Stream
516	Wantagh
315	Watertown
516	Westbury (Nassau Co.)
516	Westhampton
516	Wheatley Hills
914	White Lake
914	White Plains
914	Woodbourne
914	Woodridge
914	Woodstock
914	Yonkers
914	Yorktown Heights
NORTH CAROLINA	
919	Camp Le Jeune
704	Charlotte
919	Durham
919	Greensboro
704	Lexington
919	Raleigh
704	Salisbury
919	Wilmington
919	Winston-Salem
NORTH DAKOTA	
701	All points
OHIO	
216	Akron
216	Canton
513	Cincinnati
216	Cleveland
614	Columbus
513	Dayton
216	East Liverpool
419	Findlay
513	Hamilton
614	Lancaster
614	Marion
216	Massillon
513	Middletown
513	Norwood
614	Portsmouth
419	Sandusky
513	Springfield
614	Steubenville
419	Toledo
216	Youngstown
614	Zanesville
OKLAHOMA	
405	Oklahoma City
918	Tulsa
OREGON	
503	All points
PENNSYLVANIA	
215	Allentown (Lehigh Co.)
814	Altoona
412	Beaver Falls
814	Bellefonte
215	Bethlehem
717	Bloomsburg
814	Bradford
717	Chambersburg
717	Columbia
814	Du Bois
215	Easton
814	Erie
412	Greensburg
717	Harrisburg
717	Hazleton
412	Indiana
717	Lancaster
717	Lebanon
215	Levittown
717	Lock Haven
412	McKeesport
412	New Castle
215	Philadelphia
412	Pittsburgh
215	Pottstown

area code	location
215	Reading
412	Rochester
717	Scranton
814	State College
717	Stroudsburg
717	Sunbury
814	Uniontown (Indiana Co.)
814	Warren
412	Washington
215	Wayne
215	West Chester
717	Wilkes-Barre
717	Williamsport
RHODE ISLAND	
401	All points

area code	location
SOUTH CAROLINA	
803	All points
SOUTH DAKOTA	
605	All points
TENNESSEE	
615	Chattanooga
901	Memphis
615	Nashville
TEXAS	
915	Abilene
806	Amarillo
512	Austin
713	Beaumont
512	Brownsville

area code	location
512	Corpus Christi
214	Dallas
817	Fort Worth
713	Galveston
713	Houston
512	San Antonio
713	Texas City-La Marque
713	Wharton
UTAH	
801	All points
VERMONT	
802	All points
VIRGINIA	
703	All points

area code	location
WASHINGTON	
206	Olympia
206	Seattle
509	Spokane
206	Tacoma
509	Yakima
WEST VIRGINIA	
304	All points
WISCONSIN	
414	Appleton
715	Eau Claire
414	Green Bay
608	Madison
414	Milwaukee
414	Racine

area code	location
WYOMING	
307	All points
WIDE AREA TEL SERV	
800	All locations
PUERTO RICO	
809	All points
ALBERTA	
403	All points
BRITISH COLUMBIA	
604	All points
MANITOBA	
204	All points
NEW BRUNSWICK	
506	All points

area code	location
NOVA SCOTIA	
902	All points
ONTARIO	
807	Fort William
519	London
705	North Bay
613	Ottawa
416	Toronto
QUEBEC	
514	Montreal
418	Quebec
819	Sherbrooke
SASKATCHEWAN	
306	All points

Word Practice

Here are the new words in the last five stories you read. Check the words you remember:

___supermarket
___checkout counter
___six
___together
___bewildered
___aisles
___frozen
___cases
___hundreds
___items

___strange
___purchases
___customers
___register
___receipt
___change
___tired
___responsible

___blocks

___drugstore
___pointed
___reached
___stranger
___watched
___hurried
___question
___hurry
___neighborhood
___direction

___miss
___corner
___walked
___recipe

___lost
___Social Security card
___worry
___application

___answering
___blank
___finished
___desk
___office
___received
___safe
___afraid
___trouble
___main office

___downpour
___afternoon
___sunny
___clear
___caught
___doorways
___thunder
___lightning
___shower

___sudden
___weatherman
___traffic
___tie-ups
___following

___company
___state
___country
___California

___Maine
___Alabama
___Connecticut
___Mexico
___assigned
___Virgin Islands
___alphabetical list

Use the spaces below to write in alphabetical order the words from the previous page:

a

b

c

d

f

h

i

l

m

n

o

p

q

r

s

t

v

w

(First)
desired
Education
When
High School
Name and Location
College
Corres. School
EXPERIENCE
LAST EMPLOYER
Date
From To
Name of Company
Address
Position
Reason for Leaving
Salary
LIST THE NAMES OF THREE REFERENCES
Name
Address
Name
Address
Name
Address
Tel. No.
Tel. No.
Signature
Tel. No.

Chuck Needed References For A New Job

Chuck wanted a new job. His friend told him there was an opening at his garage for a good man. The money was more than Chuck was getting at his place.

So Chuck went to see the manager of the garage about the job. The manager asked him questions about the kind of work he could do, and where he had worked before. Chuck asked about the hours of work and how much the job paid. Everything seemed to be satisfactory.

The manager gave Chuck an application to fill out and return the next day. He said that Chuck must give the names of two persons who knew him well and would serve as references. Chuck asked his friend about this. They talked it over and decided that his teacher at the adult school and his boss where he worked would be willing to recommend him.

Chuck asked them and both said they were willing to give him a reference for the new job. Chuck put their names and addresses on the application as his references and took it to the manager of the garage.

"You can start on the job two weeks from today," the manager told Chuck.

"Thank you," said Chuck. "I'll be here."

Check the words that are in the story "Chuck Needed References For A New Job":

___new
___his
___it
___far
___men
___mare
___than
___want
___him
___if
___end
___give
___fall
___mist
___persons
___well
___bath
___pat

___now
___has
___at
___for
___man
___more
___then
___went
___ham
___of
___and
___gave
___fill
___must
___person
___wall
___both
___put

Check the words that mean MORE THAN ONE:

___job
___friends
___garage
___jobs
___man
___opening
___men
___places
___kinds
___manager
___place
___question
___kind
___managers
___hour
___hours
___questions
___application

___days
___names
___person
___name
___persons
___references
___friend
___reference
___teachers
___adult
___bosses
___week
___teacher
___weeks
___adults
___boss
___applications
___day

Check the words that mean TODAY:

___did
___wanted
___serve
___want
___said
___know
___told
___ask
___paid
___took
___decided
___seemed
___give
___asked
___went
___talked
___started
___seem
___go
___get
___recommended
___take
___served
___tell
___start
___got
___saw
___pay
___work
___new
___asked
___worked
___say
___recommend
___do
___decide
___talk
___gave
___see

Arrange the letters to make words:

n c o m d e m r e ________________
g r e m a n a ________________
w r e h e ________________
t v e r e h n i g y ________________
s e n r e c e r e f ________________
d e k o r w ________________
a n c ________________
s m a n e ________________
g o p i n e n ________________
d t e n a w ________________
w e n k ________________
d e n i r f ________________
d e k a l t ________________
h e t ________________

Put a circle around a smaller word in each of these words. Follow example:

friend	wanted
there	than
was	getting
opening	place
for	worked
manager	hours
asked	everything
where	fill
seemed	return
knew	names
willing	talked
recommend	references
told	can
needed	the

Use each of these words in a sentence:

1. opening ______________________________.
2. garage ______________________________.
3. manager ______________________________.
4. questions ______________________________.
5. satisfactory ______________________________.
6. return ______________________________.
7. references ______________________________.
8. decided ______________________________.
9. willing ______________________________.
10. recommend ______________________________.

Fill in the missing words:

Chuck wanted a new ________. His friend told him there was an ________ at his ________ for a good man. The ________ was more than Chuck was getting at his place.

So Chuck went to see the ________ of the ________ about the ______. The manager ________ him ________ about the kind of work he could do, and ________ he had worked ______. Chuck asked about the ________ of work and how much the job ________. Everything seemed to be ________.

The ________ gave Chuck an ________ to fill out and return the next ________. He said that Chuck must give the names of two ________ who knew him well and would serve as ________. Chuck asked his friend about this. They talked it over and ______ that his teacher at the ______ school and his boss where he ______ would be ________ to ________ him.

Chuck asked them and both said they were ________ to give him a ________ for the new job. Chuck put their names and addresses on the ________ as his ______ and took it to the manager of the ______.

"You can ________ on the job two weeks from ________," the manager told Chuck.

"Thank you," said Chuck. "I'll be ________."

Joyce Needed A Social Security Card

Joyce needed a Social Security card. She was twenty-eight years old and had never been employed. Joyce had been on welfare for many years because she was not strong and had no family. Now she felt strong enough to try to get a job.

Joyce went to the adult school near her home to learn to type well enough to get a job as a typist. She practiced hard and was soon able to type very well. Her teacher told Joyce that she was ready to try for a job, and that she must get a Social Security card before she could work anywhere.

Joyce went to the Social Security office and filled out an application. When she had written in all of the information she gave it to the man at the desk.

"Thank you," he said. "We will mail your card to you in a few days. Good luck."

About ten days later the card arrived in the mail. Joyce was pleased and showed the card to her typing teacher at the adult school.

"That is good," said the teacher. "You can type well enough to apply for a job. They need a typist at the "Y" down the street. Go there in the morning and see if the job is still open. Good luck."

Joyce went to the "Y" and asked about the job. She took a typing test to show how well she could type and passed it. She showed her Social Security card and got the job.

Check the words that are in the story "Joyce Needed a Social Security Card":

___card	___cord
___end	___and
___never	___ever
___hid	___had
___net	___not
___string	___strong
___got	___get
___want	___went
___type	___tape
___wall	___tall
___will	___well
___far	___for
___get	___got
___gave	___give
___man	___men
___cord	___card
___tin	___ten
___it	___at
___still	___stall

Fill in each space with one word from the three at the right:

1. Joyce needed a Social Security ____________.	check card number
2. She had never been ____________.	married ill employed
3. Joyce wanted to be a ____________.	doctor typist singer
4. She could soon ____________ very well.	type sing drive
5. Joyce was ready to try for a ____________.	job star part
6. She filled out an ____________.	order form application form
7. The ____________ arrived in the mail.	letter card magazine
8. They ____________ a typist at the "Y."	hired saw needed
9. Joyce took a ____________ test.	typing driving hearing
10. Joyce got the ____________.	book desk job

Check the words that mean YESTERDAY:

___ write	___ needed
___ mailed	___ was
___ practice	___ went
___ arrived	___ ask
___ tried	___ worked
___ type	___ fill
___ feel	___ apply
___ mail	___ saw
___ showed	___ had
___ applied	___ felt
___ passed	___ try
___ go	___ asked
___ filled	___ take
___ get	___ see
___ gave	___ typed
___ wrote	___ show
___ is	___ pleased
___ need	___ practiced
___ please	___ got
___ pass	___ learn
___ took	___ give
___ learned	___ work
___ has	___ arrive

Arrange the letters to make words:

d e e n d e ________________ l e w l ________________

c i t u r y e s ________________ h a n e y w e r ________________

s y a r e ________________ c e f i f o ________________

r e f a l e w ________________ l i w l ________________

g r o n s t ________________ d r a c ________________

l i a m f y ________________ c l u k ________________

h e n g o u ________________ l a i m ________________

s t i t y p ________________ p l a p y ________________

Put a circle around a smaller word in each of these words. Follow example:

years	office	welfare
card	fill	many
she	man	now
needed	your	the
learn	days	near
practiced	pleased	told
was	good	that
well	said	ready
teacher	they	anywhere
down	still	when
there	open	information
morning	asked	passed
showed	show	

Use each of these words in a sentence:

1. needed ____.
2. twenty-eight ____.
3. never ____.
4. employed ____.
5. welfare ____.
6. strong ____.
7. adult ____.
8. typist ____.
9. practiced ____.
10. anywhere ____.
11. application ____.
12. information ____.
13. enough ____.
14. passed ____.
15. test ____.
16. Social Security card _____________________________________.

Fill in the missing words:

Joyce __________ a __________ Security card. She was twenty-eight ________ old and had never been ______________. Joyce had been on ____________ for many years because she was not __________ and had no family. Now she felt strong __________ to try to get a ______.

Joyce went to the __________ school near her home to learn to _____ well enough to get a job as a ____________. She __________ hard and was soon able to type very _______. Her _______ told Joyce that she was _______ to try for a job, and that she must get a Social Security __________ before she could work anywhere.

Joyce went to the Social ________ office and filled out an __________. When she had __________ in all of the _______ she gave it to the man at the desk.

"Thank you," he said. "We will ___ your _______ to you in a few days. Good luck."

About ten _____ later the _______ arrived in the _______. Joyce was __________ and showed the _______ to her _____ teacher at the _______ school.

"That is good," said the teacher. "You can _______ well enough to try for a _______. They need a ________ at the "Y" down the street. Go there in the ________________ and see if the job is still open. Good luck."

Joyce went to the "Y" and asked about the ___. She took a ________ test to show how ___ she could type and __________ it. She ________ her Social Security __________ and got the __________.

George Watched A TV Show

George liked to watch a TV show every Friday evening. The show went on right after dinner. It was a panel show with four panel members who tried to answer questions sent in by viewers.

Last Friday the panel was asked to name the ten largest cities in the United States. That meant the cities with the largest population. The panel members tried hard, but not one could name all of the ten cities. Two got eight of the cities correct, but got the other two wrong. The other panel members gave up.

George thought he could name the ten cities. He wrote them on a piece of paper while the panel members were trying. When the panel gave up and the host of the program read the correct ten cities, George found that he had written nine of the ten cities on his list. He had done better than the panel members.

Here is the correct list of the ten cities in the United States with the largest number of people: New York City (New York), Chicago (Illinois), Los Angeles (California), Philadelphia (Pennsylvania), Detroit (Michigan), Houston (Texas), Baltimore (Maryland), Dallas (Texas), Washington, D.C. and Cleveland (Ohio).

Check the words that are in the story "George Watched a TV Show":

___liked	___looked
___witch	___watch
___in	___on
___at	___it
___lost	___last
___tan	___ten
___on	___in
___but	___bat
___ill	___all
___got	___get
___give	___gave
___thought	___think
___wore	___were
___read	___read
___has	___his
___bitter	___better
___then	___than
___last	___list
___as	___is

Check the words that mean MORE THAN ONE:

___viewers
___Fridays
___question
___papers
___it
___pieces
___shows
___dinner
___panel
___member
___show
___dinners
___viewer
___ten
___city
___every
___Friday
___hosts
___lists
___people

___panels
___members
___questions
___name
___cities
___names
___one
___all
___two
___paper
___eight
___them
___piece
___person
___host
___programs
___nine
___list
___program

Put a circle around a smaller word in each of these words. Follow example:

show	than
every	Friday
four	was
viewers	panel
asked	states
the	meant
largest	with
not	other
one	them
name	when
trying	better
that	here

Arrange the letters to make words:

c h a t w ________________	p l a e n ________________
s w o h ________________	s r m e b e m ________________
n i v e e n g ________________	t i g l h ________________
r i t h g ________________	t r o c c e r ________________
a s n e r w ________________	c e p i e ________________
v i r s e e w ________________	t o h s ________________
m a n e ________________	t a p o l o i n u p ________________

Check the words that mean TODAY:

___do

___find

___was

___did

___liked

___is

___mean

___sent

___gave

___named

___like

___go

___went

___try

___wrote

___got

___watch

___ask

___meant

___give

___name

___went

___asked

___get

___watched

___did

___found

___send

___write

___tried

Use each of these words in a sentence:

1. George ______________________________.
2. watch ______________________________.
3. evening ______________________________.
4. panel show ______________________________.
5. member ______________________________.
6. nine ______________________________.
7. viewers ______________________________.
8. largest ______________________________.
9. population ______________________________.
10. cities ______________________________.
11. correct ______________________________.
12. wrong ______________________________.
13. host ______________________________.
14. list ______________________________.
15. better ______________________________.
16. people ______________________________.
17. Friday ______________________________.
18. answer ______________________________.
19. four ______________________________.
20. ten ______________________________.

Fill in the missing words:

George liked to ________ a TV show every __________ evening. The show went on right after __________. It was a ________ show with ______ panel ________ who tried to answer questions sent in by ___________.

Last Friday the ______ was asked to name the ten ______ cities in the United States. That ________ the cities with the largest __________. The panel members tried hard, but not one could name all of the ________ cities. Two got ___ of the cities ______ , but got the other two __________. The other __________ members gave up.

George thought he could ______ the ___ cities. He ______ them on a piece of paper while the panel _______________ were trying. When the ________ gave up and the ________ of the ________ read the ______ ten cities, George found that he had written ________ of the ten cities on his ________. He had done __________ than the panel ___________.

Here is the ________ list of the ten cities in the United States with the __________ number of people:

_____________________, _____________________, _____________________,

_____________________, _____________________, _____________________,

_____________________, _____________________, _____________________

and _____________________.

Enjoy doing this crossword puzzle:

DOWN:

1. Biggest.
2. Comes before ten.
3. Reply.
4. A part.
5. More than one person.

ACROSS:

4. All of the people.
6. A TV __________ show.
7. Comes after nine.

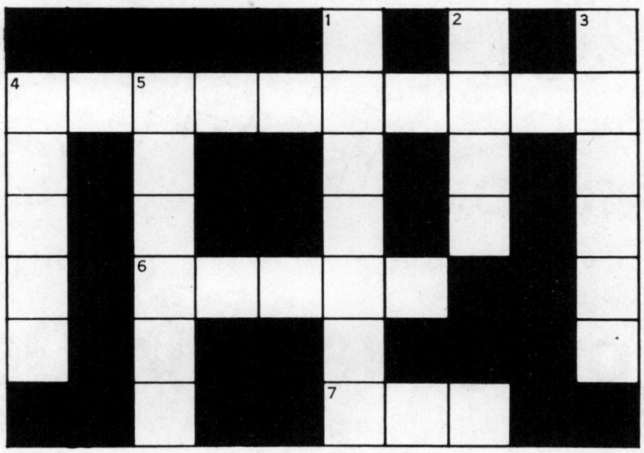
1
2
3
4
5
6
7

ZODIAC
GLASSES
WEIGHT
HEADACHE
ANYWHERE
TELEPHONE
TIRED
WRITE
TOGETHER
PRACTICE
SWEATER
WELFARE
AREA
REPAIR
ENOUGH
TRIED
RIGHT
BREAK
SOUP
FLEET
DOWNPOUR
LOAN
BELIEVE
WORRIED

Do You Believe In Devils?

Here are one hundred devils. They are really words that people have trouble spelling when they write. They are called devils because the spelling of these words troubles, annoys, or bothers people when they have to use them in writing.

The one hundred devils are listed here in alphabetical order. Ask someone to read these words out loud, one at a time, while you write them on a piece of paper. Then check the list with what you wrote to see if you have spelled all of the words correctly.

Make a list of any of the words you did not spell correctly. These are the words you need to practice, so that you can spell them correctly the next time you need to write them.

Think a minute and write on a piece of paper any words you can think of that are not on the list. Also list any words whose spellings you are not sure of. Look up each word in a dictionary, then practice writing it so that you can learn how to spell it correctly.

Check the words you know you can spell correctly.
Practice those you cannot spell correctly:

___ache
___again
___always
___among
___annoys
___answer
___any
___been
___beginning
___believe
___blue
___bread
___break
___built
___business
___busy
___buy
___can't
___choose
___color
___coming
___cough
___could
___country
___dear

___doctor
___does
___done
___don't
___early
___easy
___enough
___every
___February
___forty
___friend
___grammar
___guess
___half
___having
___hear
___heard
___here
___hoarse
___hour
___instead
___just
___knew
___know
___laid

___learn
___loose
___lose
___making
___many
___meant
___minute
___much
___none
___often
___once
___piece
___practice
___raise
___read
___ready
___said
___says
___seems
___separate
___shoes
___straight
___sugar
___sure
___their

___there
___they
___though
___through
___tired
___tonight
___too
___trouble
___truly
___Tuesday
___two
___used
___very
___wear
___Wednesday
___week
___where
___whether
___which
___whole
___women
___won't
___write
___writing
___wrote

Can you use devil words in talking, in reading and in writing? Write sentences of your own using devil words. You can use as many devil words in one sentence as you wish.

1. ____.

2. ____.

3. ____.

4. ____.

5. ____.

6. ____.

7. ____.

8. ____.

9. ____.

10. ____.

Count how many devil words you used in your sentences and write the total number here. ____________

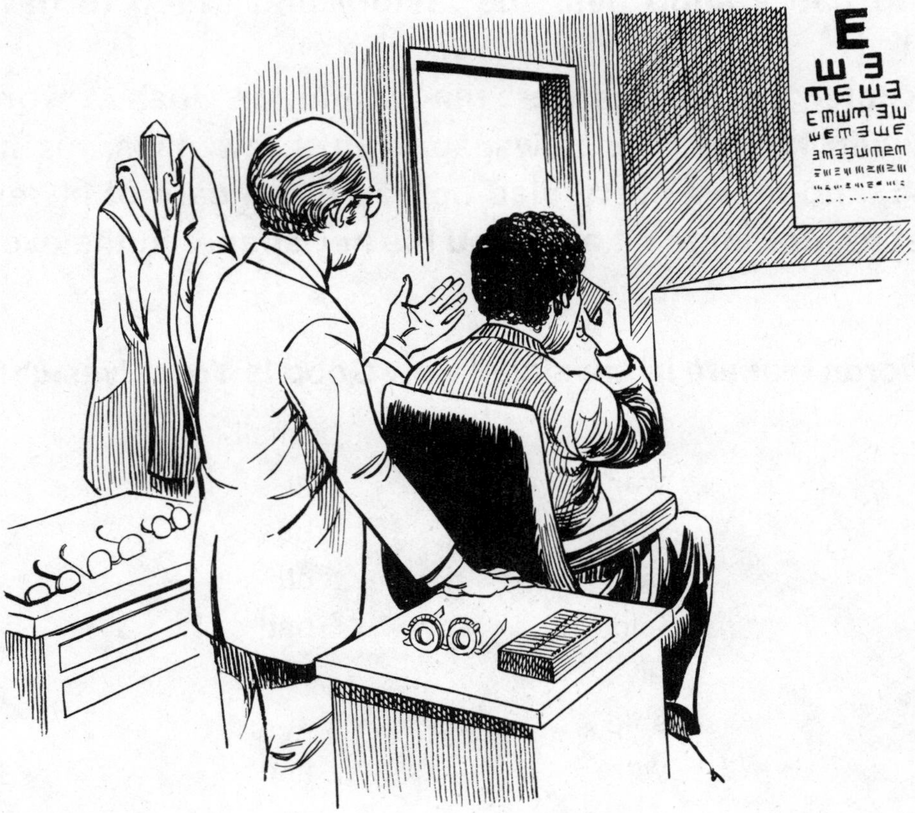

How Good Is Your Eyesight?

Mr. Joshua worked as a label examiner in a small factory. He used his eyes all day reading the labels.

At the end of the day, Mr. Joshua often had a headache over his eyes. When he sat down to read his newspaper at home, he found it hard to see the print clearly. He was worried. He decided to visit an optometrist to find out if he needed glasses.

Mr. Joshua went to see Dr. Hardy who lived in his neighborhood. Dr. Hardy tested his eyesight and examined his eyes carefully. He told Mr. Joshua that he was straining his eyes with so much close reading on the job and that he needed glasses. The glasses would prevent eyestrain, and his headaches would clear up. Dr. Hardy gave Mr. Joshua a prescription for a pair of glasses. Mr. Joshua took the prescription to an optician who had a shop near the factory and asked to have glasses made.

A week later the glasses were ready, and Mr. Joshua wore them at work and when he read his newspaper. In a few days, his headaches disappeared, and he was very glad he had taken care of his eyesight. It was a pleasure for him to sit and read his newspaper in the evening after work.

Check the words that are in the story "How Good Is Your Eyesight?":

___smell	___of	___small	___if
___as	___want	___is	___went
___his	___loved	___has	___lived
___ill	___tasted	___all	___tested
___hod	___end	___had	___and
___sit	___give	___sat	___gave
___it	___ship	___at	___shop
___fund	___wore	___find	___were

Fill in each space with one word from the three at the right:

1. Mr. Joshua works in a small ________________.	factory store restaurant
2. He uses his eyes all day to read ______________.	books magazines labels
3. After work Mr. Joshua often had a ___________.	cold drink headache
4. He could not see the newspaper ______________ clearly.	print pictures comics

5. He _______________ visit an optometrist. — decided to / hated to / wouldn't

6. Dr. Hardy tested his _______________. — hearing / eyesight / class

7. Mr. Joshua was _______________ his eyes. — resting / using / straining

8. So he got a prescription for _______________. — pills / his head / glasses

9. Then his headaches _______________. — disappeared / worsened / improved

10. Now it was a _______________ for him to read. — chore / pleasure / gas

Put a circle around a smaller word in each of these words. Follow example:

sm(all)	close	often
used	clear	when
eyes	had	was
headache	them	decided
down	care	needed
newspaper	days	his
clearly	care	neighborhood
optometrist	disappeared	eyesight
glasses	taken	carefully
lived	evening	that
tested	pleasure	eyestrain
examined	reading	pair
told	labels	made
straining	the	near

Check the words that mean YESTERDAY:

___worked	___need
___wore	___needed
___used	___go
___asked	___found
___had	___disappear
___told	___visit
___sit	___lived
___gave	___decide
___find	___examine
___prevented	___was
___saw	___cleared
___clear	___see
___is	___prevent
___examined	___found
___decided	___give
___live	___sat
___visited	___tell
___disappeared	___has
___find	___ask
___went	___use
___work	___wear

Check the words that mean ONE:

___label	___labels
___evening	___factory
___factories	___jobs
___week	___pair
___examiner	___days
___shop	___homes
___eyes	___opticians
___optician	___eye
___day	___examiners
___pairs	___prescriptions
___headaches	___headache
___prescription	___shops
___job	___weeks
___neighborhoods	___glass
___newspaper	___newspapers
___home	___evenings
___optometrist	___optometrists
___glasses	___neighborhood

Check the words that mean more than ONE:

___label	___labels
___factories	___factory
___examiner	___examiners
___eyes	___eye
___day	___days
___headaches	___headache
___newspaper	___newspapers
___home	___homes
___optometrist	___optometrists
___glasses	___glass
___neighborhood	___neighborhoods
___jobs	___job
___prescriptions	___prescription
___pair	___pairs
___opticians	___opticians
___shops	___shop
___weeks	___week
___evenings	___evening

Arrange the letters to make words:

t a c f o r y ________________	t h g i s e y e ________________
m a l s l ________________	m e t r i o p t o s t ____________
b a l e l s ________________	f u l l c a r e y ______________
d a c h e h e a ______________	s e s s a l g ________________
t n i r p ________________	s c r i p r e p i o n t __________
d r i e r o w ________________	a n i c i t o p ________________
c i d e d e d ________________	p n w e s p e a r ______________
s i v i t ________________	r o w k ________________

Use each of these words in a sentence:

1. eyesight ____________________.
2. label ____________________.
3. factory ____________________.
4. examined ____________________.
5. eyes ____________________.
6. reading ____________________.
7. headache ____________________.
8. clearly ____________________.
9. print ____________________.
10. worried ____________________.
11. decided ____________________.
12. optometrist ____________________.
13. glasses ____________________.
14. eyestrain ____________________.
15. prevent ____________________.
16. prescription ____________________.
17. pair ____________________.
18. optician ____________________.
19. disappeared ____________________.
20. pleasure ____________________.

Fill in the missing words:

Mr. Joshua worked as a __________ examiner in a small ____________. He used his _________ all day ___________ the __________.

At the end of the day, Mr. Joshua often had a ______________ over his __________. When he sat down to read his _____________ at home he found it hard to see the _________ clearly. He was _________. He _________ to visit an ________________ to find out if he needed _________.

Mr. Joshua went to see Dr. Hardy who lived in his _______________. Dr. Hardy ___________ his ___________ and examined his eyes ______________. He told Mr. Joshua that he was ________________ his eyes with so much ___________ reading on the job and that he needed ___________. The glasses would prevent ____________________ , and his ___________ would _______ up. Dr. Hardy gave Mr. Joshua a ______________ for a ___________ of glasses. Mr. Joshua took the prescription to an ____________ who had a ___________ near the _____________ and asked to have _____________ made.

A week later the ____________ were ready, and Mr. Joshua wore them at work and when he read his __________. In a few days, his _____________ disappeared, and he was very glad he has taken care of his ____________. It was a ______________ for him to sit and read his ________________ in the _______________ after work.

Word Practice

Here are the new words in the last stories you read. Check the words you remember:

___opening
___garage
___manager
___questions
___satisfactory
___return
___references
___decided
___willing
___recommend
____
___needed
___twenty-eight
___employed
___welfare
___strong
___typist
___practiced
___anywhere

___application
___information
___enough
___test
____
___panel show
___members
___nine
___viewers
___largest
___cities
___correct
___wrong
___host
___better
___Friday
___four
___ten
___population

___eyesight
___factory
___label
___examiner
___eyes
___reading
___headache
___clearly
___print
___worried
___optometrist
___glasses
___eyestrain
___prevent
___prescription
___pair
___optician
___disappeared
___pleasure

Use the spaces below to write in alphabetical order the words from the previous page:

a

______

______

b

______

c

______

______

______

d

______

______

e

______

______

______

______

______

______

f

______

______

______

g

______

______

h

______

______

i

______

l

______

______

m

______

______

n

______

______

o

______

______

______

p

______

______

______

______

______

______

______

______

q

______

r

______

______

______

______

s

______

______

t

______

______

______

______

v

______

w

______

______

______

______

1/3 OFF
ON ALL
TVs
SOLD

Mr. And Mrs. Gilson Buy A TV Set

Mr. and Mrs. Gilson decided to buy a TV set. A reliable store advertised a sale of TV sets at reasonable prices. They went to the store and looked at several sets. They also looked at the prices and finally picked out a set they liked at a price they could afford.

The salesman asked, "How do you want to pay for the TV set? Cash or monthly payments?"

"We will make monthly payments. How much will we have to pay each month?" asked Mr. Gilson.

The salesman figured it out and told Mr. Gilson he must make a down payment of $25 and sign an agreement to pay a small amount each month for the next eleven months. Mr. Gilson asked exactly how much of each payment was interest and how much money was for the TV set. The salesman wrote down the exact amount for interest charges and for the payments and gave the paper to Mr. Gilson.

Then Mr. Gilson signed the contract and gave the salesman $25 in cash for the down payment. The salesman gave him a receipt for the cash payment and a copy of the contract.

The TV set was delivered to their home before the weekend. Mr. and Mrs. Gilson and some friends spent many hours that weekend enjoying programs on the new TV set.

Check the words that are in the story "Mr. and Mrs. Gilson Buy a TV Set":

___boy	___buy
___set	___sat
___sale	___sole
___it	___at
___want	___went
___stare	___store
___sits	___sets
___packed	___picked
___well	___will
___mist	___must
___mike	___make
___than	___then
___small	___smell
___far	___for
___write	___wrote
___for	___far
___give	___gave
___same	___some
___now	___new

Fill in each space with one word from the three at the right:

1.	The Gilson's wanted a ______________ set.	furniture TV game
2.	They went to the ______________ to buy a set.	airport store office
3.	They found a set they could ______________.	borrow afford rent
4.	Mrs. Gilson had to sign a ______________.	contract letter check
5.	He made a ______________ payment of $25.	late down complete
6.	Part of each payment was ______________.	free interest gold
7.	The ______________ gave Mr. Gilson a receipt.	salesman cashier teller
8.	The TV set was ______________ to their home.	mailed flown delivered
9.	They got it before the ______________.	weekend game deadline
10.	Everybody enjoyed the ______________ they saw.	music words programs

Put a circle around a smaller word in each of these words. Follow example:

decided	advertised
reasonable	sale
the	price
also	looked
they	picked
liked	salesman
monthly	asked
payments	want
told	will
then	figured
and	enjoying
money	agreement
eleven	small
for	exactly
charges	interest
signed	down
was	before
their	delivered
hours	weekend
programs	many

Check the words that mean MORE THAN ONE:

___store	___copies
___sale	___payments
___program	___agreement
___weekends	___homes
___sets	___contract
___receipt	___month
___hours	___amount
___charges	___salesmen
___price	___paper
___papers	___friends
___friend	___charge
___amounts	___prices
___salesman	___receipts
___copy	___hour
___months	___weekend
___contracts	___set
___home	___sales
___agreements	___program
___payment	___stores

Check the words that mean TODAY:

___ went
___ like
___ gave
___ look
___ deliver
___ signed
___ decide
___ is
___ spend
___ ask
___ buy
___ liked
___ advertise
___ tell
___ enjoy
___ figured
___ made
___ advertised
___ picked
___ go
___ pick
___ delivered

___ enjoyed
___ give
___ write
___ wanted
___ decided
___ bought
___ was
___ wrote
___ asked
___ afford
___ mailed
___ sign
___ told
___ pay
___ looked
___ figure
___ make
___ want
___ afforded
___ paid
___ wrote
___ spent

Arrange the letters to make words:

b l e r e l i a ________________

l e s a ________________

c e r i p ________________

e l b a n a s o e r ________________

a l l i n y f ________________

d r o f f a ________________

s h a c ________________

m e n s p a y t ________________

g i f r u e d ________________

g i n s ________________

v e n e l e ________________

t e r i n s t e ________________

g e s r a h c ________________

t c a r t n o c ________________

e i p t c e r ________________

o p y c ________________

Use each of these words in a sentence:

1. decided ________________.
2. reliable ________________.
3. reasonable ________________.
4. several ________________.
5. afford ________________.
6. salesman ________________.
7. monthly ________________.
8. figured ________________.
9. agreement ________________.
10. eleven ________________.
11. exactly ________________.
12. interest ________________.
13. charges ________________.
14. contract ________________.
15. receipt ________________.
16. copy ________________.
17. weekend ________________.

Fill in the missing words:

Mr. and Mrs. Gilson __________ to buy a TV set. A __________ store __________ a __________ of TV sets at __________ prices. They went to the store and looked at __________ sets. They also __________ at the prices and finally __________ out a set they liked at a __________ they could __________.

The __________ asked, "How do you want to pay for the TV set? Cash or monthly __________?"

"We will make __________ payments. How much will we have to pay each __________?" asked Mr. Gilson.

The __________ figured it out and told Mr. Gilson he must make a down __________ of $25 and sign an __________ to pay a small __________ each month for the next __________ months. Mr. Gilson asked __________ how much of each __________ was __________ and how much money was for the TV set. The salesman wrote down the __________ amount for __________ charges and for the payments and gave the __________ to Mr. Gilson.

Then Mr. Gilson __________ the __________ and gave the salesman $25 in cash for the __________ payment. The salesman gave him a __________ for the cash __________ and a copy of the __________.

The TV set was __________ to their home before the __________. Mr. and Mrs. Gilson and some friends spent many __________ that __________ enjoying __________ on the new TV set.

The Casserole

My sister Annie was given a cookbook by a friend. When I went to her house, Annie and I looked through the cookbook together. We wanted to find a new recipe and cook something special for dinner that night. We found a recipe that we thought we would like to use. It is called a casserole. Annie has a dish in which to make a casserole. She bought it at a sale in the shopping center. Here is the recipe:

1 pound ground beef
1 small can tomato paste
1 small can tomato sauce
1 tablespoon dry onion soup mix
½ cup water
½ box noodles, cooked
1 small carton cottage cheese
1 small carton sour cream

Crumble the beef in a skillet. Cook slowly over low heat for 3 minutes. Drain off the grease. Add tomato paste, sauce, onion mix and water. Bring to a boil. Cover and simmer 20 minutes. Mix cottage cheese and sour cream in a bowl.

Put half the beef mixture in a casserole. Add half the noodles. Cover with half the cheese and cream mixture. Do this again. Bake in hot oven 25-30 minutes until it bubbles. Makes 4 servings.

Check the words that are in the story "The Casserole":

___want	___went
___new	___now
___far	___for
___lake	___like
___dash	___dish
___sole	___sale
___it	___at
___small	___smell
___soap	___soup
___cap	___cup
___law	___low
___bail	___boil
___end	___and
___put	___pat
___on	___in
___hat	___hot
___fund	___find

Fill in each space with one word from the three at the right:

1. My sister was given a _______________.	house cookbook car
2. We looked through the cookbook _______________.	yesterday quickly together
3. We wanted to find a new _______________.	food recipe story
4. We wanted something _______________ for dinner.	special hot light
5. We decided to make a _______________.	stew pie casserole
6. We needed a casserole _______________.	oven dish glass
7. We used one pound of ground _______________.	beef pork veal
8. We also used one can of tomato _______________.	soup juice sauce
9. We cooked the caserole in the _______________.	toaster oven broiler
10. We had enough food for _______________ people.	three two four

Check the words that mean YESTERDAY:

___thought
___go
___used
___do
___simmered
___like
___had
___called
___made
___bought
___baked
___cover
___want
___bring
___found
___crumbled
___drain
___is
___bubbled
___cooked
___mixed
___add

___cook
___bubble
___was
___added
___mix
___find
___brought
___wanted
___drain
___think
___buy
___makes
___call
___wanted
___covered
___bake
___simmer
___did
___has
___liked
___went
___use

Check the words that mean ONE:

___ cookbooks	___ tablespoons
___ friend	___ carton
___ houses	___ cheeses
___ recipe	___ skillet
___ dinner	___ minutes
___ oven	___ pounds
___ mixtures	___ shopping center
___ serving	___ sale
___ bowl	___ noodles
___ onions	___ night
___ nights	___ sauce
___ noodle	___ onion
___ sales	___ bowls
___ shopping centers	___ servings
___ pound	___ mixture
___ sauces	___ ovens
___ minute	___ dinners
___ skillets	___ recipes
___ cheese	___ house
___ cartons	___ friends
___ tablespoon	___ cookbook
___ can	___ cans

Put a circle around a smaller word in each of these words. Follow example:

given	friend
when	together
looked	and
wanted	for
something	she
called	shopping
sale	center
here	can
ground	tomato
small	paste
tablespoon	cup
onion	cottage
cooked	carton
cheese	cream
sour	slowly
skillet	drain
heat	cookbook
off	boil
bring	minutes
bowl	again
mixture	

Arrange the letters to make words:

n e g i v ________	l e t l i s k ________
g h o t h r u ________	b l e c r u m ________
p i c e r e ________	n a i r d ________
l e r o s e s a c ________	s v r g s i n e ________
t r e n e c ________	r e m m i s ________
t e s p a ________	l o w b ________
m a t o o t ________	b b l e s b u ________
l e d s n o o ________	s u n m i t e ________

Use each of these words in a sentence:

1. sister ________.
2. special ________.
3. casserole ________.
4. dish ________.
5. center ________.
6. shopping ________.
7. pound ________.
8. ground ________.
9. tomato ________.
10. paste ________.
11. sauce ________.
12. onion ________.
13. tablespoon ________.
14. noodles ________.
15. carton ________.
16. cottage cheese ________.
17. sour cream ________.
18. crumble ________.
19. skillet ________.
20. grease ________.
21. simmer ________.
22. bubbles ________.
23. half ________.

Fill in the missing words:

My sister Annie was given a __________ by a __________. When I went to her ______, Annie and I looked ________ the __________ together. We wanted to find a new __________ and cook something special for dinner that __________. We found a ______ we thought we would like to __________. It is called a __________. Annie has a __________ in which to make a casserole. She bought it at a ______________ in the shopping ______________. Here is the ______________:

1 __________ ground beef

1 small ______ tomato paste

1 __________ can __________ sauce

1 ____________ dry ______ soup mix

½ ______ water

½ box ____________, cooked

1 small __________ cottage __________

1 ________ carton ________ cream

__________ the beef in a __________. Cook slowly over low ________ for 3 ________. Drain off the ______. Add tomato ________, sauce, __________ mix and water. Bring to a ________. Cover and __________ 20 _______. Mix cottage ___ and ______ cream in a ______. Put half the ________ mixture in a __________. Add half the ______. Cover with half the __________ and cream __________. Do this again. Bake in hot __________ 25-30 __________ until it __________. Makes 4 __________.

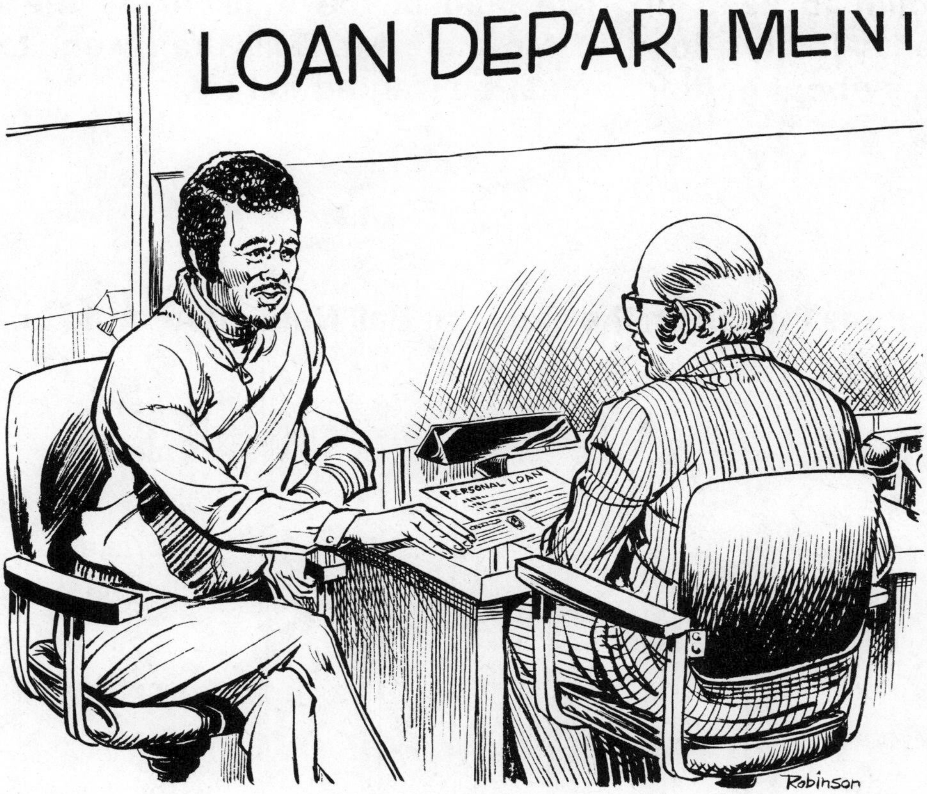
LOAN DEPARTMENT
PERSONAL LOAN
Robinson

Al Ball Needed An Auto Loan

Al Ball needed a loan to buy a new car. His old car broke down completely, and it was not worth the cost to have it repaired. Mr. Ball saw a sign in his bank offering loans for autos, home improvements and education. The next time he went to the bank, Mr. Ball went to the loan department to ask about a loan. He took his savings bankbook and other identification with him. He had his Social Security card, his union card, his driver's license, his library card, and his enrollment card at the adult school.

The man at the loan department asked Mr. Ball several questions to see if he was eligible for a loan. Mr. Ball met all of the requirements needed to get a loan. He was over eighteen years of age. He had been in the same job for more than two years. He had only one other debt and it was a small one. He still owed four payments on his TV set. He was earning enough money so that the monthly payments would not be too much for him to keep up. The man at the bank made the necessary arrangements for the loan to Mr. Ball. Mr. Ball then went to the auto dealer to see about getting the car he wanted to buy.

Check the words that are in the story "Al Ball Needed An Auto Loan":

___buy	___bay
___now	___new
___has	___his
___broke	___brake
___down	___dawn
___end	___and
___net	___not
___cost	___cast
___sew	___saw
___met	___meet
___fir	___for
___time	___tame
___want	___went
___ham	___him
___hid	___had
___car	___card
___stall	___still
___set	___sat
___not	___net
___get	___got
___more	___mare
___ill	___all

Fill in each space with one word from the three at the right:

1. Al Ball needed a ____________.	plant pencil loan
2. His ____________ car broke down completely.	old red father's
3. The ____________ was offering loans.	supermarket bank diner
4. Mr. Ball ____________ about a loan.	asked wrote called
5. He took his ____________ to the bank.	wife son identification
6. He also ____________ his savings bankbook.	lost took forgot
7. Mr. Ball met all of the ____________.	people requirements children
8. He was earning ____________ money.	little no enough
9. He was ____________ for a loan.	eligible wishing singing
10. Mr. Ball went to the auto ____________.	dealer garage show

Put a circle around a smaller word in each of these words. Follow example:

needed	dealer
loan	the
down	repaired
completely	his
autos	offering
went	improvements
other	department
had	and
card	man
asked	was
requirements	years
eighteen	same
been	one

Check the words that mean TODAY:

___want	___wanted
___need	___needed
___got	___get
___bought	___buy
___keep	___kept
___owe	___owed
___broke	___break
___is	___was
___repaired	___repair
___was	___is
___have	___had
___see	___saw
___offer	___offered
___took	___take
___asked	___ask
___go	___went

Check the words that mean MORE THAN ONE:

___loan
___cars
___signs
___bank
___auto
___requirements
___question
___dealers
___arrangement
___payments
___homes
___improvement
___time
___department
___bankbooks
___cards
___debt
___years
___schools
___adult
___license
___unions

___licenses
___union
___year
___adults
___school
___bankbook
___card
___times
___departments
___improvements
___dealer
___payment
___requirement
___arrangements
___debts
___home
___autos
___banks
___loans
___car
___sign
___question

Check the words that mean ONE:

___ loan	___ loans
___ cars	___ car
___ signs	___ sign
___ bank	___ banks
___ auto	___ autos
___ homes	___ home
___ improvement	___ improvements
___ time	___ times
___ department	___ departments
___ books	___ book
___ cards	___ card
___ union	___ unions
___ licenses	___ license
___ adults	___ adult
___ school	___ schools
___ year	___ years
___ debts	___ debt
___ payment	___ payments
___ arrangements	___ arrangement
___ dealer	___ dealers
___ questions	___ question
___ requirement	___ requirements

Arrange the letters to make words:

p a i r r e ____________

o r t h e ____________

e l b i g i l e ____________

t e b d ____________

l e r d e a ____________

t e e n h g i e ____________

s g n i v a s ____________

i t o s n s e u q ____________

n a o l ____________

k e b r o ____________

Use each of these words in a sentence:

1. loan ____________.
2. broke ____________.
3. completely ____________.
4. several ____________.
5. payments ____________.
6. worth ____________.
7. repair ____________.
8. offering ____________.
9. improvements ____________.
10. education ____________.
11. savings ____________.
12. identification ____________.
13. enrollment ____________.
14. questions ____________.
15. eligible ____________.
16. requirements ____________.
17. eighteen ____________.
18. debt ____________.
19. arrangements ____________.
20. dealer ____________.

Fill in the missing words:

Al Ball needed a __________ to buy a new car. His old car __________ down __________, and was not __________ the cost to have it __________. Mr. Ball saw a sign in his bank __________ loans for autos, home __________ and __________. The next time he went to the bank, Mr. Ball went to the loan department to ask about a __________. He took his __________ bankbook and other __________ with him. He had his Social Security card, his union card, his driver's __________, his library card, and his __________ card at the adult school.

The man at the loan department asked Mr. Ball several __________ to see if he was __________ for a loan. Mr. Ball met all of the __________ to get a loan. He was over __________ years of age. He had been in the same job for more than two years. He had only one other __________ and it was a small one. He still owed four __________ on his TV set. He was earning enough money so that the __________ payments would not be too much for him to keep up. The man at the bank made the necessary __________ for the loan to Mr. Ball. Mr. Ball then went to the auto __________ to see about getting the __________ he wanted to buy.

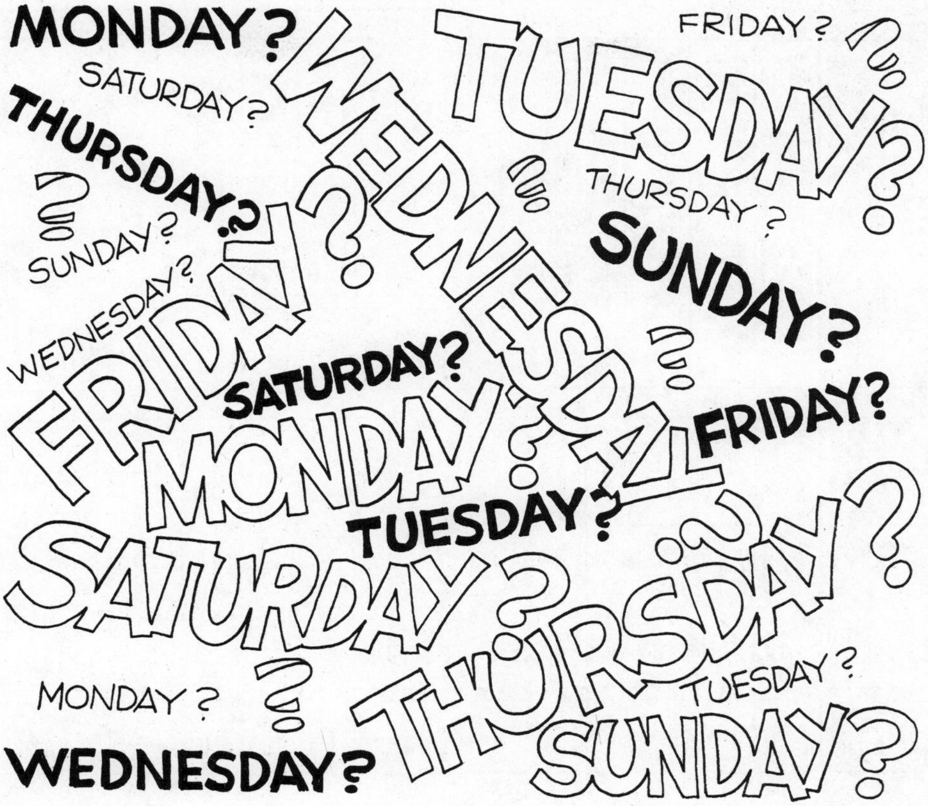
MONDAY?
SATURDAY?
THURSDAY?
SUNDAY?
WEDNESDAY?
FRIDAY?
WEDNESDAY?
TUESDAY?
FRIDAY?
THURSDAY?
SUNDAY?
SATURDAY?
MONDAY?
FRIDAY?
TUESDAY?
SATURDAY?
THURSDAY?
MONDAY?
TUESDAY?
WEDNESDAY?
SUNDAY?

What Day Were You Born?

If you do not know, perhaps you can find out by looking at the perpetual calendar on the next page. A perpetual calendar is very different from a regular calendar. A perpetual calendar makes it possible to figure out the day of the week for any given date over many years. It can be very helpful if you need to know the day something happened many years ago.

If you do know the day on which you were born, you can read the poem below and see if the description applies to you. If you know the day that anyone else was born—your children or grandchildren, for example—you can enjoy the poem.

Monday's child is FAIR OF FACE,
Tuesday's child is FULL OF GRACE,
Wednesday's child is FULL OF WOE,
Thursday's child HAS FAR TO GO,
Friday's child is LOVING AND GIVING,
Saturday's child WORKS HARD FOR A LIVING,
Sunday's child is FAIR, WISE, GOOD AND GAY.

1800... 4	1826... 1	1852...12	1878... 3	1904...13	1930... 4	1956... 8	1982... 6	2008...10	2034... 1
1801... 5	1827... 2	1853... 7	1879... 4	1905... 1	1931... 5	1957... 3	1983... 7	2009... 5	2035... 2
1802... 6	1828...10	1854... 1	1880...12	1906... 2	1932...13	1958... 4	1984... 8	2010... 6	2036...10
1803... 7	1829... 5	1855... 2	1881... 7	1907... 3	1933... 1	1959... 5	1985... 3	2011... 7	2037... 5
1804... 8	1830... 6	1856...10	1882... 1	1908...11	1934... 2	1960...13	1986... 4	2012... 8	2038... 6
1805... 3	1831... 7	1857... 5	1883... 2	1909... 6	1935... 3	1961... 1	1987... 5	2013... 3	2039... 7
1806... 4	1832... 8	1858... 6	1884...10	1910... 7	1936...11	1962... 2	1988...13	2014... 4	2040... 8
1807... 5	1833... 3	1859... 7	1885... 5	1911... 1	1937... 6	1963... 3	1989... 1	2015... 5	2041... 3
1808...13	1834... 4	1860... 8	1886... 6	1912... 9	1938... 7	1964...11	1990... 2	2016...13	2042... 4
1809... 1	1835... 5	1861... 3	1887... 7	1913... 4	1939... 1	1965... 6	1991... 3	2017... 1	2043... 5
1810... 2	1836...13	1862... 4	1888... 8	1914... 5	1940... 9	1966... 7	1992...11	2018... 2	2044...13
1811... 3	1837... 1	1863... 5	1889... 3	1915... 6	1941... 4	1967... 1	1993... 6	2019... 3	2045... 1
1812...11	1838... 2	1864...13	1890... 4	1916...14	1942... 5	1968... 9	1994... 7	2020...11	2046... 2
1813... 6	1839... 3	1865... 1	1891... 5	1917... 2	1943... 6	1969... 4	1995... 1	2021... 6	2047... 3
1814... 7	1840...11	1866... 2	1892...13	1918... 3	1944...14	1970... 5	1996... 9	2022... 7	2048...11
1815... 1	1841... 6	1867... 3	1893... 1	1919... 4	1945... 2	1971... 6	1997... 4	2023... 1	2049... 6
1816... 9	1842... 7	1868...11	1894... 2	1920...12	1946... 3	1972...14	1998... 5	2024... 9	2050... 7
1817... 4	1843... 1	1869... 6	1895... 3	1921... 7	1947... 4	1973... 2	1999... 6	2025... 4	2051... 1
1818... 5	1844... 9	1870... 7	1896...11	1922... 1	1948...12	1974... 3	2000...14	2026... 5	2052... 9
1819... 6	1845... 4	1871... 1	1897... 6	1923... 2	1949... 7	1975... 4	2001... 2	2027... 6	2053... 4
1820...14	1846... 5	1872... 9	1898... 7	1924...10	1950... 1	1976...12	2002... 3	2028...14	2054... 5
1821... 2	1847... 6	1873... 4	1899... 1	1925... 5	1951... 2	1977... 7	2003... 4	2029... 2	2055... 6
1822... 3	1848...14	1874... 5	1900... 2	1926... 6	1952...10	1978... 1	2004...12	2030... 3	2056...14
1823... 4	1849... 2	1875... 6	1901... 3	1927... 7	1953... 5	1979... 2	2005... 7	2031... 4	2057... 2
1824...12	1850... 3	1876...14	1902... 4	1928... 8	1954... 6	1980...10	2006... 1	2032...12	2058... 3
1825... 7	1851... 4	1877... 2	1903... 5	1929... 3	1955... 7	1981... 5	2007... 2	2033... 7	2059... 4

1

Month	S M T W T F S
JANUARY	1 2 3 4 5 6 7 / 8 9 10 11 12 13 14 / 15 16 17 18 19 20 21 / 22 23 24 25 26 27 28 / 29 30 31
FEBRUARY	1 2 3 4 / 5 6 7 8 9 10 11 / 12 13 14 15 16 17 18 / 19 20 21 22 23 24 25 / 26 27 28
MARCH	1 2 3 4 / 5 6 7 8 9 10 11 / 12 13 14 15 16 17 18 / 19 20 21 22 23 24 25 / 26 27 28 29 30 31
APRIL	1 / 2 3 4 5 6 7 8 / 9 10 11 12 13 14 15 / 16 17 18 19 20 21 22 / 23 24 25 26 27 28 29 / 30
MAY	1 2 3 4 5 6 / 7 8 9 10 11 12 13 / 14 15 16 17 18 19 20 / 21 22 23 24 25 26 27 / 28 29 30 31
JUNE	1 2 3 / 4 5 6 7 8 9 10 / 11 12 13 14 15 16 17 / 18 19 20 21 22 23 24 / 25 26 27 28 29 30
JULY	1 / 2 3 4 5 6 7 8 / 9 10 11 12 13 14 15 / 16 17 18 19 20 21 22 / 23 24 25 26 27 28 29 / 30 31
AUGUST	1 2 3 4 5 / 6 7 8 9 10 11 12 / 13 14 15 16 17 18 19 / 20 21 22 23 24 25 26 / 27 28 29 30 31
SEPTEMBER	1 2 / 3 4 5 6 7 8 9 / 10 11 12 13 14 15 16 / 17 18 19 20 21 22 23 / 24 25 26 27 28 29 30
OCTOBER	1 2 3 4 5 6 7 / 8 9 10 11 12 13 14 / 15 16 17 18 19 20 21 / 22 23 24 25 26 27 28 / 29 30 31
NOVEMBER	1 2 3 4 / 5 6 7 8 9 10 11 / 12 13 14 15 16 17 18 / 19 20 21 22 23 24 25 / 26 27 28 29 30
DECEMBER	1 2 / 3 4 5 6 7 8 9 / 10 11 12 13 14 15 16 / 17 18 19 20 21 22 23 / 24 25 26 27 28 29 30 / 31

2 — 1973

Month	S M T W T F S
JANUARY	1 2 3 4 5 6 / 7 8 9 10 11 12 13 / 14 15 16 17 18 19 20 / 21 22 23 24 25 26 27 / 28 29 30 31
FEBRUARY	1 2 3 / 4 5 6 7 8 9 10 / 11 12 13 14 15 16 17 / 18 19 20 21 22 23 24 / 25 26 27 28
MARCH	1 2 3 / 4 5 6 7 8 9 10 / 11 12 13 14 15 16 17 / 18 19 20 21 22 23 24 / 25 26 27 28 29 30 31
APRIL	1 2 3 4 5 6 7 / 8 9 10 11 12 13 14 / 15 16 17 18 19 20 21 / 22 23 24 25 26 27 28 / 29 30
MAY	1 2 3 4 5 / 6 7 8 9 10 11 12 / 13 14 15 16 17 18 19 / 20 21 22 23 24 25 26 / 27 28 29 30 31
JUNE	1 2 / 3 4 5 6 7 8 9 / 10 11 12 13 14 15 16 / 17 18 19 20 21 22 23 / 24 25 26 27 28 29 30
JULY	1 2 3 4 5 6 7 / 8 9 10 11 12 13 14 / 15 16 17 18 19 20 21 / 22 23 24 25 26 27 28 / 29 30 31
AUGUST	1 2 3 4 / 5 6 7 8 9 10 11 / 12 13 14 15 16 17 18 / 19 20 21 22 23 24 25 / 26 27 28 29 30 31
SEPTEMBER	1 / 2 3 4 5 6 7 8 / 9 10 11 12 13 14 15 / 16 17 18 19 20 21 22 / 23 24 25 26 27 28 29 / 30
OCTOBER	1 2 3 4 5 6 / 7 8 9 10 11 12 13 / 14 15 16 17 18 19 20 / 21 22 23 24 25 26 27 / 28 29 30 31
NOVEMBER	1 2 3 / 4 5 6 7 8 9 10 / 11 12 13 14 15 16 17 / 18 19 20 21 22 23 24 / 25 26 27 28 29 30
DECEMBER	1 / 2 3 4 5 6 7 8 / 9 10 11 12 13 14 15 / 16 17 18 19 20 21 22 / 23 24 25 26 27 28 29 / 30 31

3

Month	S M T W T F S
JANUARY	1 2 3 4 5 / 6 7 8 9 10 11 12 / 13 14 15 16 17 18 19 / 20 21 22 23 24 25 26 / 27 28 29 30 31
FEBRUARY	1 2 / 3 4 5 6 7 8 9 / 10 11 12 13 14 15 16 / 17 18 19 20 21 22 23 / 24 25 26 27 28
MARCH	1 2 / 3 4 5 6 7 8 9 / 10 11 12 13 14 15 16 / 17 18 19 20 21 22 23 / 24 25 26 27 28 29 30 / 31
APRIL	1 2 3 4 5 6 / 7 8 9 10 11 12 13 / 14 15 16 17 18 19 20 / 21 22 23 24 25 26 27 / 28 29 30
MAY	1 2 3 4 / 5 6 7 8 9 10 11 / 12 13 14 15 16 17 18 / 19 20 21 22 23 24 25 / 26 27 28 29 30 31
JUNE	1 / 2 3 4 5 6 7 8 / 9 10 11 12 13 14 15 / 16 17 18 19 20 21 22 / 23 24 25 26 27 28 29 / 30
JULY	1 2 3 4 5 6 / 7 8 9 10 11 12 13 / 14 15 16 17 18 19 20 / 21 22 23 24 25 26 27 / 28 29 30 31
AUGUST	1 2 3 / 4 5 6 7 8 9 10 / 11 12 13 14 15 16 17 / 18 19 20 21 22 23 24 / 25 26 27 28 29 30 31
SEPTEMBER	1 2 3 4 5 6 7 / 8 9 10 11 12 13 14 / 15 16 17 18 19 20 21 / 22 23 24 25 26 27 28 / 29 30
OCTOBER	1 2 3 4 5 / 6 7 8 9 10 11 12 / 13 14 15 16 17 18 19 / 20 21 22 23 24 25 26 / 27 28 29 30 31
NOVEMBER	1 2 / 3 4 5 6 7 8 9 / 10 11 12 13 14 15 16 / 17 18 19 20 21 22 23 / 24 25 26 27 28 29 30
DECEMBER	1 2 3 4 5 6 7 / 8 9 10 11 12 13 14 / 15 16 17 18 19 20 21 / 22 23 24 25 26 27 28 / 29 30 31

4

Month	S M T W T F S
JANUARY	1 2 3 4 / 5 6 7 8 9 10 11 / 12 13 14 15 16 17 18 / 19 20 21 22 23 24 25 / 26 27 28 29 30 31
FEBRUARY	1 / 2 3 4 5 6 7 8 / 9 10 11 12 13 14 15 / 16 17 18 19 20 21 22 / 23 24 25 26 27 28
MARCH	1 / 2 3 4 5 6 7 8 / 9 10 11 12 13 14 15 / 16 17 18 19 20 21 22 / 23 24 25 26 27 28 29 / 30 31
APRIL	1 2 3 4 5 / 6 7 8 9 10 11 12 / 13 14 15 16 17 18 19 / 20 21 22 23 24 25 26 / 27 28 29 30
MAY	1 2 3 / 4 5 6 7 8 9 10 / 11 12 13 14 15 16 17 / 18 19 20 21 22 23 24 / 25 26 27 28 29 30 31
JUNE	1 2 3 4 5 6 7 / 8 9 10 11 12 13 14 / 15 16 17 18 19 20 21 / 22 23 24 25 26 27 28 / 29 30
JULY	1 2 3 4 5 / 6 7 8 9 10 11 12 / 13 14 15 16 17 18 19 / 20 21 22 23 24 25 26 / 27 28 29 30 31
AUGUST	1 2 / 3 4 5 6 7 8 9 / 10 11 12 13 14 15 16 / 17 18 19 20 21 22 23 / 24 25 26 27 28 29 30 / 31
SEPTEMBER	1 2 3 4 5 6 / 7 8 9 10 11 12 13 / 14 15 16 17 18 19 20 / 21 22 23 24 25 26 27 / 28 29 30
OCTOBER	1 2 3 4 / 5 6 7 8 9 10 11 / 12 13 14 15 16 17 18 / 19 20 21 22 23 24 25 / 26 27 28 29 30 31
NOVEMBER	1 / 2 3 4 5 6 7 8 / 9 10 11 12 13 14 15 / 16 17 18 19 20 21 22 / 23 24 25 26 27 28 29 / 30
DECEMBER	1 2 3 4 5 6 / 7 8 9 10 11 12 13 / 14 15 16 17 18 19 20 / 21 22 23 24 25 26 27 / 28 29 30 31

5

Month	S M T W T F S
JANUARY	1 2 3 / 4 5 6 7 8 9 10 / 11 12 13 14 15 16 17 / 18 19 20 21 22 23 24 / 25 26 27 28 29 30 31
FEBRUARY	1 2 3 4 5 6 7 / 8 9 10 11 12 13 14 / 15 16 17 18 19 20 21 / 22 23 24 25 26 27 28
MARCH	1 2 3 4 5 6 7 / 8 9 10 11 12 13 14 / 15 16 17 18 19 20 21 / 22 23 24 25 26 27 28 / 29 30 31
APRIL	1 2 3 4 / 5 6 7 8 9 10 11 / 12 13 14 15 16 17 18 / 19 20 21 22 23 24 25 / 26 27 28 29 30
MAY	1 2 / 3 4 5 6 7 8 9 / 10 11 12 13 14 15 16 / 17 18 19 20 21 22 23 / 24 25 26 27 28 29 30 / 31
JUNE	1 2 3 4 5 6 / 7 8 9 10 11 12 13 / 14 15 16 17 18 19 20 / 21 22 23 24 25 26 27 / 28 29 30
JULY	1 2 3 4 / 5 6 7 8 9 10 11 / 12 13 14 15 16 17 18 / 19 20 21 22 23 24 25 / 26 27 28 29 30 31
AUGUST	1 / 2 3 4 5 6 7 8 / 9 10 11 12 13 14 15 / 16 17 18 19 20 21 22 / 23 24 25 26 27 28 29 / 30 31
SEPTEMBER	1 2 3 4 5 / 6 7 8 9 10 11 12 / 13 14 15 16 17 18 19 / 20 21 22 23 24 25 26 / 27 28 29 30
OCTOBER	1 2 3 / 4 5 6 7 8 9 10 / 11 12 13 14 15 16 17 / 18 19 20 21 22 23 24 / 25 26 27 28 29 30 31
NOVEMBER	1 2 3 4 5 6 7 / 8 9 10 11 12 13 14 / 15 16 17 18 19 20 21 / 22 23 24 25 26 27 28 / 29 30
DECEMBER	1 2 3 4 5 / 6 7 8 9 10 11 12 / 13 14 15 16 17 18 19 / 20 21 22 23 24 25 26 / 27 28 29 30 31

6 — 1971

Month	S M T W T F S
JANUARY	1 2 / 3 4 5 6 7 8 9 / 10 11 12 13 14 15 16 / 17 18 19 20 21 22 23 / 24 25 26 27 28 29 30 / 31
FEBRUARY	1 2 3 4 5 6 / 7 8 9 10 11 12 13 / 14 15 16 17 18 19 20 / 21 22 23 24 25 26 27 / 28
MARCH	1 2 3 4 5 6 / 7 8 9 10 11 12 13 / 14 15 16 17 18 19 20 / 21 22 23 24 25 26 27 / 28 29 30 31
APRIL	1 2 3 / 4 5 6 7 8 9 10 / 11 12 13 14 15 16 17 / 18 19 20 21 22 23 24 / 25 26 27 28 29 30
MAY	1 / 2 3 4 5 6 7 8 / 9 10 11 12 13 14 15 / 16 17 18 19 20 21 22 / 23 24 25 26 27 28 29 / 30 31
JUNE	1 2 3 4 5 / 6 7 8 9 10 11 12 / 13 14 15 16 17 18 19 / 20 21 22 23 24 25 26 / 27 28 29 30
JULY	1 2 3 / 4 5 6 7 8 9 10 / 11 12 13 14 15 16 17 / 18 19 20 21 22 23 24 / 25 26 27 28 29 30 31
AUGUST	1 2 3 4 5 6 7 / 8 9 10 11 12 13 14 / 15 16 17 18 19 20 21 / 22 23 24 25 26 27 28 / 29 30 31
SEPTEMBER	1 2 3 4 / 5 6 7 8 9 10 11 / 12 13 14 15 16 17 18 / 19 20 21 22 23 24 25 / 26 27 28 29 30
OCTOBER	1 2 / 3 4 5 6 7 8 9 / 10 11 12 13 14 15 16 / 17 18 19 20 21 22 23 / 24 25 26 27 28 29 30 / 31
NOVEMBER	1 2 3 4 5 6 / 7 8 9 10 11 12 13 / 14 15 16 17 18 19 20 / 21 22 23 24 25 26 27 / 28 29 30
DECEMBER	1 2 3 4 / 5 6 7 8 9 10 11 / 12 13 14 15 16 17 18 / 19 20 21 22 23 24 25 / 26 27 28 29 30 31

7

Month	S M T W T F S
JANUARY	1 / 2 3 4 5 6 7 8 / 9 10 11 12 13 14 15 / 16 17 18 19 20 21 22 / 23 24 25 26 27 28 29 / 30 31
FEBRUARY	1 2 3 4 5 / 6 7 8 9 10 11 12 / 13 14 15 16 17 18 19 / 20 21 22 23 24 25 26 / 27 28
MARCH	1 2 3 4 5 / 6 7 8 9 10 11 12 / 13 14 15 16 17 18 19 / 20 21 22 23 24 25 26 / 27 28 29 30 31
APRIL	1 2 / 3 4 5 6 7 8 9 / 10 11 12 13 14 15 16 / 17 18 19 20 21 22 23 / 24 25 26 27 28 29 30
MAY	1 2 3 4 5 6 7 / 8 9 10 11 12 13 14 / 15 16 17 18 19 20 21 / 22 23 24 25 26 27 28 / 29 30 31
JUNE	1 2 3 4 / 5 6 7 8 9 10 11 / 12 13 14 15 16 17 18 / 19 20 21 22 23 24 25 / 26 27 28 29 30
JULY	1 2 / 3 4 5 6 7 8 9 / 10 11 12 13 14 15 16 / 17 18 19 20 21 22 23 / 24 25 26 27 28 29 30 / 31
AUGUST	1 2 3 4 5 6 / 7 8 9 10 11 12 13 / 14 15 16 17 18 19 20 / 21 22 23 24 25 26 27 / 28 29 30 31
SEPTEMBER	1 2 3 / 4 5 6 7 8 9 10 / 11 12 13 14 15 16 17 / 18 19 20 21 22 23 24 / 25 26 27 28 29 30
OCTOBER	1 / 2 3 4 5 6 7 8 / 9 10 11 12 13 14 15 / 16 17 18 19 20 21 22 / 23 24 25 26 27 28 29 / 30 31
NOVEMBER	1 2 3 4 5 / 6 7 8 9 10 11 12 / 13 14 15 16 17 18 19 / 20 21 22 23 24 25 26 / 27 28 29 30
DECEMBER	1 2 3 / 4 5 6 7 8 9 10 / 11 12 13 14 15 16 17 / 18 19 20 21 22 23 24 / 25 26 27 28 29 30 31

8

Month	S M T W T F S
JANUARY	1 2 3 4 5 6 7 / 8 9 10 11 12 13 14 / 15 16 17 18 19 20 21 / 22 23 24 25 26 27 28 / 29 30 31
FEBRUARY	1 2 3 4 / 5 6 7 8 9 10 11 / 12 13 14 15 16 17 18 / 19 20 21 22 23 24 25 / 26 27 28 29
MARCH	1 2 3 / 4 5 6 7 8 9 10 / 11 12 13 14 15 16 17 / 18 19 20 21 22 23 24 / 25 26 27 28 29 30 31
APRIL	1 2 3 4 5 6 7 / 8 9 10 11 12 13 14 / 15 16 17 18 19 20 21 / 22 23 24 25 26 27 28 / 29 30
MAY	1 2 3 4 5 / 6 7 8 9 10 11 12 / 13 14 15 16 17 18 19 / 20 21 22 23 24 25 26 / 27 28 29 30 31
JUNE	1 2 / 3 4 5 6 7 8 9 / 10 11 12 13 14 15 16 / 17 18 19 20 21 22 23 / 24 25 26 27 28 29 30
JULY	1 2 3 4 5 6 7 / 8 9 10 11 12 13 14 / 15 16 17 18 19 20 21 / 22 23 24 25 26 27 28 / 29 30 31
AUGUST	1 2 3 4 / 5 6 7 8 9 10 11 / 12 13 14 15 16 17 18 / 19 20 21 22 23 24 25 / 26 27 28 29 30 31
SEPTEMBER	1 / 2 3 4 5 6 7 8 / 9 10 11 12 13 14 15 / 16 17 18 19 20 21 22 / 23 24 25 26 27 28 29 / 30
OCTOBER	1 2 3 4 5 6 / 7 8 9 10 11 12 13 / 14 15 16 17 18 19 20 / 21 22 23 24 25 26 27 / 28 29 30 31
NOVEMBER	1 2 3 / 4 5 6 7 8 9 10 / 11 12 13 14 15 16 17 / 18 19 20 21 22 23 24 / 25 26 27 28 29 30
DECEMBER	1 / 2 3 4 5 6 7 8 / 9 10 11 12 13 14 15 / 16 17 18 19 20 21 22 / 23 24 25 26 27 28 29 / 30 31

9

Month	S M T W T F S
JANUARY	1 2 3 4 5 6 / 7 8 9 10 11 12 13 / 14 15 16 17 18 19 20 / 21 22 23 24 25 26 27 / 28 29 30 31
FEBRUARY	1 2 3 / 4 5 6 7 8 9 10 / 11 12 13 14 15 16 17 / 18 19 20 21 22 23 24 / 25 26 27 28 29
MARCH	1 2 / 3 4 5 6 7 8 9 / 10 11 12 13 14 15 16 / 17 18 19 20 21 22 23 / 24 25 26 27 28 29 30 / 31
APRIL	1 2 3 4 5 6 / 7 8 9 10 11 12 13 / 14 15 16 17 18 19 20 / 21 22 23 24 25 26 27 / 28 29 30
MAY	1 2 3 4 / 5 6 7 8 9 10 11 / 12 13 14 15 16 17 18 / 19 20 21 22 23 24 25 / 26 27 28 29 30 31
JUNE	1 / 2 3 4 5 6 7 8 / 9 10 11 12 13 14 15 / 16 17 18 19 20 21 22 / 23 24 25 26 27 28 29 / 30
JULY	1 2 3 4 5 6 / 7 8 9 10 11 12 13 / 14 15 16 17 18 19 20 / 21 22 23 24 25 26 27 / 28 29 30 31
AUGUST	1 2 3 / 4 5 6 7 8 9 10 / 11 12 13 14 15 16 17 / 18 19 20 21 22 23 24 / 25 26 27 28 29 30 31
SEPTEMBER	1 2 3 4 5 6 7 / 8 9 10 11 12 13 14 / 15 16 17 18 19 20 21 / 22 23 24 25 26 27 28 / 29 30
OCTOBER	1 2 3 4 5 / 6 7 8 9 10 11 12 / 13 14 15 16 17 18 19 / 20 21 22 23 24 25 26 / 27 28 29 30 31
NOVEMBER	1 2 / 3 4 5 6 7 8 9 / 10 11 12 13 14 15 16 / 17 18 19 20 21 22 23 / 24 25 26 27 28 29 30
DECEMBER	1 2 3 4 5 6 7 / 8 9 10 11 12 13 14 / 15 16 17 18 19 20 21 / 22 23 24 25 26 27 28 / 29 30 31

10

Month	S M T W T F S
JANUARY	1 2 3 4 5 / 6 7 8 9 10 11 12 / 13 14 15 16 17 18 19 / 20 21 22 23 24 25 26 / 27 28 29 30 31
FEBRUARY	1 2 / 3 4 5 6 7 8 9 / 10 11 12 13 14 15 16 / 17 18 19 20 21 22 23 / 24 25 26 27 28 29
MARCH	1 / 2 3 4 5 6 7 8 / 9 10 11 12 13 14 15 / 16 17 18 19 20 21 22 / 23 24 25 26 27 28 29 / 30 31
APRIL	1 2 3 4 5 / 6 7 8 9 10 11 12 / 13 14 15 16 17 18 19 / 20 21 22 23 24 25 26 / 27 28 29 30
MAY	1 2 3 / 4 5 6 7 8 9 10 / 11 12 13 14 15 16 17 / 18 19 20 21 22 23 24 / 25 26 27 28 29 30 31
JUNE	1 2 3 4 5 6 7 / 8 9 10 11 12 13 14 / 15 16 17 18 19 20 21 / 22 23 24 25 26 27 28 / 29 30
JULY	1 2 3 4 5 / 6 7 8 9 10 11 12 / 13 14 15 16 17 18 19 / 20 21 22 23 24 25 26 / 27 28 29 30 31
AUGUST	1 2 / 3 4 5 6 7 8 9 / 10 11 12 13 14 15 16 / 17 18 19 20 21 22 23 / 24 25 26 27 28 29 30 / 31
SEPTEMBER	1 2 3 4 5 6 / 7 8 9 10 11 12 13 / 14 15 16 17 18 19 20 / 21 22 23 24 25 26 27 / 28 29 30
OCTOBER	1 2 3 4 / 5 6 7 8 9 10 11 / 12 13 14 15 16 17 18 / 19 20 21 22 23 24 25 / 26 27 28 29 30 31
NOVEMBER	1 / 2 3 4 5 6 7 8 / 9 10 11 12 13 14 15 / 16 17 18 19 20 21 22 / 23 24 25 26 27 28 29 / 30
DECEMBER	1 2 3 4 5 6 / 7 8 9 10 11 12 13 / 14 15 16 17 18 19 20 / 21 22 23 24 25 26 27 / 28 29 30 31

11

Month	S M T W T F S
JANUARY	1 2 3 4 / 5 6 7 8 9 10 11 / 12 13 14 15 16 17 18 / 19 20 21 22 23 24 25 / 26 27 28 29 30 31
FEBRUARY	1 / 2 3 4 5 6 7 8 / 9 10 11 12 13 14 15 / 16 17 18 19 20 21 22 / 23 24 25 26 27 28 29
MARCH	1 2 3 4 5 6 7 / 8 9 10 11 12 13 14 / 15 16 17 18 19 20 21 / 22 23 24 25 26 27 28 / 29 30 31
APRIL	1 2 3 4 / 5 6 7 8 9 10 11 / 12 13 14 15 16 17 18 / 19 20 21 22 23 24 25 / 26 27 28 29 30
MAY	1 2 / 3 4 5 6 7 8 9 / 10 11 12 13 14 15 16 / 17 18 19 20 21 22 23 / 24 25 26 27 28 29 30 / 31
JUNE	1 2 3 4 5 6 / 7 8 9 10 11 12 13 / 14 15 16 17 18 19 20 / 21 22 23 24 25 26 27 / 28 29 30
JULY	1 2 3 4 / 5 6 7 8 9 10 11 / 12 13 14 15 16 17 18 / 19 20 21 22 23 24 25 / 26 27 28 29 30 31
AUGUST	1 / 2 3 4 5 6 7 8 / 9 10 11 12 13 14 15 / 16 17 18 19 20 21 22 / 23 24 25 26 27 28 29 / 30 31
SEPTEMBER	1 2 3 4 5 / 6 7 8 9 10 11 12 / 13 14 15 16 17 18 19 / 20 21 22 23 24 25 26 / 27 28 29 30
OCTOBER	1 2 3 / 4 5 6 7 8 9 10 / 11 12 13 14 15 16 17 / 18 19 20 21 22 23 24 / 25 26 27 28 29 30 31
NOVEMBER	1 2 3 4 5 6 7 / 8 9 10 11 12 13 14 / 15 16 17 18 19 20 21 / 22 23 24 25 26 27 28 / 29 30
DECEMBER	1 2 3 4 5 / 6 7 8 9 10 11 12 / 13 14 15 16 17 18 19 / 20 21 22 23 24 25 26 / 27 28 29 30 31

12

Month	S M T W T F S
JANUARY	1 2 3 / 4 5 6 7 8 9 10 / 11 12 13 14 15 16 17 / 18 19 20 21 22 23 24 / 25 26 27 28 29 30 31
FEBRUARY	1 2 3 4 5 6 7 / 8 9 10 11 12 13 14 / 15 16 17 18 19 20 21 / 22 23 24 25 26 27 28 / 29
MARCH	1 2 3 4 5 6 / 7 8 9 10 11 12 13 / 14 15 16 17 18 19 20 / 21 22 23 24 25 26 27 / 28 29 30 31
APRIL	1 2 3 / 4 5 6 7 8 9 10 / 11 12 13 14 15 16 17 / 18 19 20 21 22 23 24 / 25 26 27 28 29 30
MAY	1 / 2 3 4 5 6 7 8 / 9 10 11 12 13 14 15 / 16 17 18 19 20 21 22 / 23 24 25 26 27 28 29 / 30 31
JUNE	1 2 3 4 5 / 6 7 8 9 10 11 12 / 13 14 15 16 17 18 19 / 20 21 22 23 24 25 26 / 27 28 29 30
JULY	1 2 3 / 4 5 6 7 8 9 10 / 11 12 13 14 15 16 17 / 18 19 20 21 22 23 24 / 25 26 27 28 29 30 31
AUGUST	1 2 3 4 5 6 7 / 8 9 10 11 12 13 14 / 15 16 17 18 19 20 21 / 22 23 24 25 26 27 28 / 29 30 31
SEPTEMBER	1 2 3 4 / 5 6 7 8 9 10 11 / 12 13 14 15 16 17 18 / 19 20 21 22 23 24 25 / 26 27 28 29 30
OCTOBER	1 2 / 3 4 5 6 7 8 9 / 10 11 12 13 14 15 16 / 17 18 19 20 21 22 23 / 24 25 26 27 28 29 30 / 31
NOVEMBER	1 2 3 4 5 6 / 7 8 9 10 11 12 13 / 14 15 16 17 18 19 20 / 21 22 23 24 25 26 27 / 28 29 30
DECEMBER	1 2 3 4 / 5 6 7 8 9 10 11 / 12 13 14 15 16 17 18 / 19 20 21 22 23 24 25 / 26 27 28 29 30 31

13

Month	S M T W T F S
JANUARY	1 2 / 3 4 5 6 7 8 9 / 10 11 12 13 14 15 16 / 17 18 19 20 21 22 23 / 24 25 26 27 28 29 30 / 31
FEBRUARY	1 2 3 4 5 6 / 7 8 9 10 11 12 13 / 14 15 16 17 18 19 20 / 21 22 23 24 25 26 27 / 28 29
MARCH	1 2 3 4 5 / 6 7 8 9 10 11 12 / 13 14 15 16 17 18 19 / 20 21 22 23 24 25 26 / 27 28 29 30 31
APRIL	1 2 / 3 4 5 6 7 8 9 / 10 11 12 13 14 15 16 / 17 18 19 20 21 22 23 / 24 25 26 27 28 29 30
MAY	1 2 3 4 5 6 7 / 8 9 10 11 12 13 14 / 15 16 17 18 19 20 21 / 22 23 24 25 26 27 28 / 29 30 31
JUNE	1 2 3 4 / 5 6 7 8 9 10 11 / 12 13 14 15 16 17 18 / 19 20 21 22 23 24 25 / 26 27 28 29 30
JULY	1 2 / 3 4 5 6 7 8 9 / 10 11 12 13 14 15 16 / 17 18 19 20 21 22 23 / 24 25 26 27 28 29 30 / 31
AUGUST	1 2 3 4 5 6 / 7 8 9 10 11 12 13 / 14 15 16 17 18 19 20 / 21 22 23 24 25 26 27 / 28 29 30 31
SEPTEMBER	1 2 3 / 4 5 6 7 8 9 10 / 11 12 13 14 15 16 17 / 18 19 20 21 22 23 24 / 25 26 27 28 29 30
OCTOBER	1 / 2 3 4 5 6 7 8 / 9 10 11 12 13 14 15 / 16 17 18 19 20 21 22 / 23 24 25 26 27 28 29 / 30 31
NOVEMBER	1 2 3 4 5 / 6 7 8 9 10 11 12 / 13 14 15 16 17 18 19 / 20 21 22 23 24 25 26 / 27 28 29 30
DECEMBER	1 2 3 / 4 5 6 7 8 9 10 / 11 12 13 14 15 16 17 / 18 19 20 21 22 23 24 / 25 26 27 28 29 30 31

14 — 1972

Month	S M T W T F S
JANUARY	1 / 2 3 4 5 6 7 8 / 9 10 11 12 13 14 15 / 16 17 18 19 20 21 22 / 23 24 25 26 27 28 29 / 30 31
FEBRUARY	1 2 3 4 5 / 6 7 8 9 10 11 12 / 13 14 15 16 17 18 19 / 20 21 22 23 24 25 26 / 27 28 29
MARCH	1 2 3 4 / 5 6 7 8 9 10 11 / 12 13 14 15 16 17 18 / 19 20 21 22 23 24 25 / 26 27 28 29 30 31
APRIL	1 / 2 3 4 5 6 7 8 / 9 10 11 12 13 14 15 / 16 17 18 19 20 21 22 / 23 24 25 26 27 28 29 / 30
MAY	1 2 3 4 5 6 / 7 8 9 10 11 12 13 / 14 15 16 17 18 19 20 / 21 22 23 24 25 26 27 / 28 29 30 31
JUNE	1 2 3 / 4 5 6 7 8 9 10 / 11 12 13 14 15 16 17 / 18 19 20 21 22 23 24 / 25 26 27 28 29 30
JULY	1 / 2 3 4 5 6 7 8 / 9 10 11 12 13 14 15 / 16 17 18 19 20 21 22 / 23 24 25 26 27 28 29 / 30 31
AUGUST	1 2 3 4 5 / 6 7 8 9 10 11 12 / 13 14 15 16 17 18 19 / 20 21 22 23 24 25 26 / 27 28 29 30 31
SEPTEMBER	1 2 / 3 4 5 6 7 8 9 / 10 11 12 13 14 15 16 / 17 18 19 20 21 22 23 / 24 25 26 27 28 29 30
OCTOBER	1 2 3 4 5 6 7 / 8 9 10 11 12 13 14 / 15 16 17 18 19 20 21 / 22 23 24 25 26 27 28 / 29 30 31
NOVEMBER	1 2 3 4 / 5 6 7 8 9 10 11 / 12 13 14 15 16 17 18 / 19 20 21 22 23 24 25 / 26 27 28 29 30
DECEMBER	1 2 / 3 4 5 6 7 8 9 / 10 11 12 13 14 15 16 / 17 18 19 20 21 22 23 / 24 25 26 27 28 29 30 / 31

DIRECTIONS: Pick desired year from box at top left. The number shown with each year indicates what calendar to use for that year.

Check the words that are in the story "What Day Were You Born?":

___know	___knew
___if	___of
___week	___work
___were	___wore
___burn	___born
___net	___not
___figure	___figures
___fund	___find
___locking	___looking
___calendar	___colander
___in	___on
___were	___wore
___new	___now
___prescription	___description
___pair	___fair

Fill in each space with one word from the three at the right:

1. Monday's child is fair of ______________.	face lace trace
2. Tuesday's child is full of ______________.	place grace pace
3. Wednesday's child is full of ______________.	hoe toe woe
4. Thursday's child has far to ______________.	so no go
5. Friday's child is loving and ______________.	living giving waving
6. Saturday's child works hard for a ____________.	giving living diving
7. Sunday's child is fair, wise, good, and ________.	gay may say
8. See if the ______________ applies to you.	story description information

Check the words that mean ONE:

___day ___calendars

___weeks ___week

___calendar ___days

___descriptions ___woes

___ranges ___graces

___dates ___years

___pages ___page

___poem ___children

___child ___poems

___year ___description

___grace ___date

___woe ___range

___grandchildren ___faces

___face ___grandchild

Check the words that indicate YESTERDAY:

___ is	___ did
___ knew	___ enjoyed
___ are	___ applied
___ happened	___ was
___ need	___ happen
___ find	___ saw
___ look	___ applies
___ figure	___ enjoy
___ know	___ needed
___ were	___ do
___ found	___ figured
___ looked	___ made
___ see	___ make

Put a circle around a smaller word in each of these words. Follow example:

what	your
know	looking
can	calendar
below	almanac
children	the
fair	now
grace	anyone
not	grandchildren
find	face
description	works
examples	good
enjoy	wise
this	born
perpetual	figure
	range

Arrange the letters to make words:

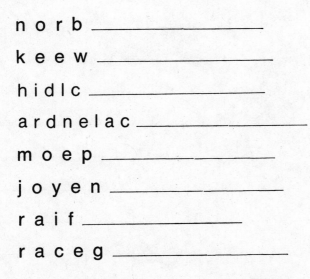

n o r b ____________________

k e e w ____________________

h i d l c ____________________

a r d n e l a c ____________________

m o e p ____________________

j o y e n ____________________

r a i f ____________________

r a c e g ____________________

Make these into words:

u g i e r f ____________________

l a r u g e r ____________________

e t a d ____________________

e s i w ____________________

f l u h l p e ____________________

o r k s w ____________________

e o w ____________________

w e l f ____________________

Use each of these words in a sentence:

1. week ____________________.
2. born ____________________.
3. perpetual calendar ____________________.
4. library ____________________.
5. poem ____________________.
6. enjoy ____________________.
7. description ____________________.
8. applies ____________________.
9. anyone ____________________.
10. grandchildren ____________________.
11. loving ____________________.
12. helpful ____________________.
13. possible ____________________.
14. wise ____________________.
15. full of grace ____________________.
16. fair of face ____________________.

Fill in the missing words:

If you do not know, ________________ you can find out by looking at the perpetual ________________ on the next ________________. A perpetual calendar is very different from a ________________ calendar. A perpetual ________________ makes it possible to ________________ out the day of the ________________ for any ________________ date over many ________________. It can be very ________________ if you need to know the ________________ something ________________ many years ago.

If you do ________________ the day on ________________ you were ________________, you can read the ________________ below and see if the ________________ applies to you. If you ________________ the day that ________________ else was born—your children or ________________, for example—you can enjoy the poem.

Monday's child is fair of ________________,
Tuesday's child is full of ________________,
Wednesday's ________________ is full of ________________,
Thursday's child has ________________ to ________________,
Friday's child is ________________ and giving,
Saturday's child works ________________ for a ________________,
Sunday's child is ________, wise, ________, and gay.

Enjoy doing this crossword puzzle:

DOWN

1. Front part of your head.
2. Your birthday is the day you were ____________.
3. There are seven days in a ________.
6. I ____________ a home.

ACROSS

4. Study the perpetual ________.
5. I __________ the day on which I was born.
7. Friday's child is loving and __________.

1
2
3
4
5
6
7

Word Practice

Here are the new words in the last stories you read. Check the words you remember:

___decided
___reliable
___reasonable
___several
___afford
___salesman
___monthly
___figured
___agreement
___eleven
___exact
___interest
___charges
___contract
___receipt
___copy
___weekend

___sister
___special
___casserole
___center
___shopping
___pound
___ground

___tomato
___paste
___sauce
___onion
___tablespoon
___noodles
___carton
___cottage cheese
___sour cream
___crumble
___skillet
___grease
___simmer
___bubbles
___half

___loan
___broke
___completely
___worth
___repaired
___offering
___improvements
___education
___identification

___eligible
___enrollment
___questions
___requirements
___eighteen
___debt
___arrangements
___dealer

___born
___perpetual calendar
___different
___loving
___poem
___description
___applies
___anyone
___grandchildren
___figure
___range
___full of grace
___fair of face
___woe
___wide

Use the spaces below to write in alphabetical order the words from the previous page:

a

e

m

s

n

o

b

f

p

t

c

g

w

q

h

r

i

d

l

Here are 231 words that you have read in this book. Check the words you remember.

a

___address
___afford
___afraid
___afternoon
___agreement
___aisles
___Alabama
___alphabetical list
___another
___answering
___anyone
___anywhere
___application
___applies
___arrangements
___asked
___assigned
___assistance

b

___better
___bewildered
___blank
___block
___boil
___born
___broke
___bubbles
___business

c

___California
___carefully
___carton
___casserole
___caught
___center
___change
___charges
___cheaper
___checkout
___cities
___clear
___clearly
___company
___completely
___condensed soup
___contract
___corner
___cost
___cottage cheese
___counter
___country
___county
___creamed
___customers

d

___dealer
___debt
___decided
___delayed
___delivered
___description
___desk
___dial
___direction
___disappeared
___doorways
___downpour
___drop
___drugstore

e

___education
___eligible
___employed
___employees
___enough
___enrollment
___envelope
___everyone
___exact
___examiner
___expensive
___eyes
___eyesight
___eyestrain

f

___factory
___fair of face
___fasten
___figures
___finished
___first
___following
___four
___frozen
___full of grace

g

___garage
___given
___glasses
___good
___grandchildren
___grease
___ground

h

___half
___headache
___help
___host
___hundreds
___hurried
___hurries

i

___identification
___improvement
___included
___information
___interest
___interesting
___items

l

___label
___large
___largest
___left hand corner
___legibly
___letter
___lightning
___list
___loan
___local
___long distance
___lost

m

___mail
___Maine
___main office
___manager
___member
___Mexico
___miss
___mixture
___monthly

n

___name
___needed
___neighborhood
___nephew
___next
___nine
___noodles
___number

o

___offering
___onion
___opening
___operator
___optician
___optometrist

p

___pair
___panel show
___paper
___parsley
___perpetual calendar
___pieces
___pleasure
___poem
___pointed
___population
___possible
___postage
___postcard

___population
___pound
___practiced
___prescription
___print
___purchases
___put

q
___questions
___quickly

r
___reading
___reasonable
___recipe
___recommend
___register
___relatives
___repair
___requirements
___responsible
___return

s
___safe
___salesman
___salt
___satisfactory
___sauce
___saucepan
___sealed
___serve
___several
___sheet
___shopping
___shower
___simmer
___six
___skillet
___soup
___sour cream
___special
___started
___stranger
___stronger
___sudden
___sunny
___supermarket
___sweater

t
___tablespoon
___tarragon
___telephone
___ten
___test
___tired
___thunder
___tomato
___total
___traffic
___trouble

v
___viewers
___Virgin Islands

w
___walked
___watch
___watched
___wear
___weatherman
___weekend
___welfare
___willing
___window
___with
___without
___word
___worried
___wrong

z
___zip code

WORD GAME

Many small words can be made from large words. There are more than twenty small words in the following word: CALENDAR. Can you find six small words? Write them down. See how many more you can find. Follow example:

C A L E N D A R

1. D E A R ____________ 5. ____________

2. ____________ 6. ____________

3 ____________ 7. ____________

4. ____________ 8. ____________

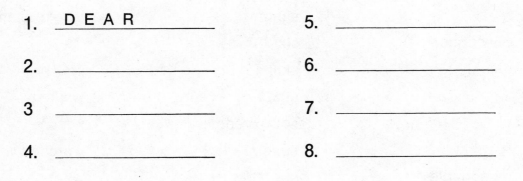

Try this word. There are about twenty small words in this word: WEDNESDAY. Can you find ten or more small words? Write them down. Follow example:

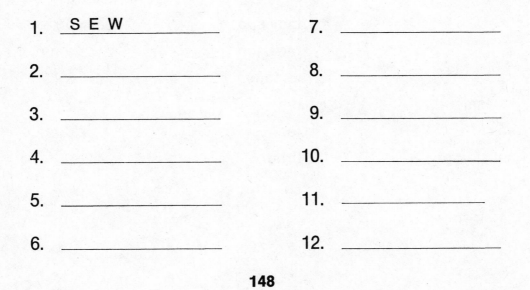

W E D N E S D A Y

1. S E W ____________ 7. ____________

2. ____________ 8. ____________

3. ____________ 9. ____________

4. ____________ 10. ____________

5. ____________ 11. ____________

6. ____________ 12. ____________